Survey Research

 ESSENTIAL RESOURCES FOR SOCIAL RESEARCH

Series Editor: Keith F Punch, University of Western Australia

A series of short practical 'how-to' books aimed at the beginning researcher. The books will cover a central topic, including the main methods, approaches and analytic techniques in social research, from developing a research topic through to writing and presenting research results. Each book is designed to be used as an independent guide or as a workbook to accompany Keith Punch's bestselling textbook *An Introduction to Social Research: Quantitative & Qualitative Approaches* (Sage, 1998).

Survey Research

The Basics

Keith F Punch

SAGE Publications
Los Angeles • London • New Delhi • Singapore

© Keith F Punch 2003

First published 2003
Reprinted 2005, 2007

SAGE Publications Ltd.
1 Oliver's Yard
55 City Road
London EC1Y 1SP

SAGE Publications Inc
2455 Teller Road
Thousand Oaks, California 91320

SAGE Publications India Pvt Ltd.
B1/I 1 Mohan Cooperative Industrial Area
Mathura Road, New Delhi 110 044
India

SAGE Publications Asia-Pacific Pte Ltd
33 Pekin Street #02-01
Far East Square
Singapore 048763

British Library Cataloguing in Publication data

A catalogue record for this book is available from the British Library

ISBN 978-0-7619-4704-2 (hbk)
ISBN 978-0-7619-4705-9 (pbk)

Library of Congress Control Number: 2002114574

Contents

List of Tables

List of Boxes

Preface

Introduction to Social Research (Punch, 1998: 76–83) dealt in general terms with the topic of the correlational survey, or the quantitative-survey-relating-variables. This book develops the topic in greater detail, aiming both to show the logic of the survey and to offer hands-on advice to student researchers preparing such surveys as projects or dissertations. It is the second book in the series *Essential Resources for Social Research*. The first was *Developing Effective Research Proposals* (Punch, 2000).

The focus here is on the quantitative-survey-relating-variables, the essential idea of which is that a sample of people will be measured across a number of variables, using a self-report questionnaire, and the resulting quantitative data will be used to study relationships between the variables. Of course this is only one type of survey. But I believe it to be the most common type, especially among student projects. Whether that is true or not, the knowledge gained from a detailed understanding of this type of survey transfers to other types of survey.

The book therefore aims to build a thorough understanding of the logic of this type of survey, and to offer hands-on advice as to how to conduct one. It unpacks the survey to show what the elements and the issues are on a logical basis. In line with this, therefore, the survey method is not 'theorised' to any great extent, and technical issues are not overly stressed. Of course, numerous technical issues underlie the logic. Because I have wanted to keep these as far as possible out of the text, I have suggested further reading on key technical issues in Appendix 1.

Once again, I want to thank the research students and researchers I have worked with over the years. I also want to thank John West, Barry Sheridan and Russell Waugh, colleagues who have helped in different ways with the content of this book, and Myra Taylor who helped with the index. Robyn Wilson has again been of great assistance in the preparation of the manuscript, and Zoe Elliott, Michael Carmichael and the team at Sage Publications (UK) have as usual been most supportive and a pleasure to work with.

Once again, too, I would welcome feedback on this book.

1

Introduction and Purpose

CONTENTS

1.1 FOCUS AND PURPOSE OF THIS BOOK

The survey has long been a central strategy in social research. However, the term 'survey' itself is very broad, covering many different types, and it is used in many different ways and in many different contexts. Because of this, there already exists a great deal of literature on survey methods, some of it general and some of it focused on surveys in particular types of situation. A new book on surveys therefore needs to have a distinct focus based on a clear rationale.

This book focuses on small-scale quantitative surveys which study the relationships between variables. The reason for the focus on quantitative-surveys-relating-variables is that this method is central to a very wide range of social science research, but is not often dealt with directly, and as a whole, in the literature. The reason for the focus on small-scale surveys is that the book is aimed at graduate students in a research training environment where very often only small-scale surveys are possible.

Of course, not all surveys are quantitative. Qualitative surveys, usu-ally asking open-ended questions, do not normally produce quantitative or numerical data. People respond with answers to these open-ended questions in words, and researchers often proceed to analyse such responses without somehow transforming the words into numbers. Such surveys are not included in this book, which deals only with surveys designed around quantitative data.

The essence of quantitative research is the study of relationships between variables. For the quantitative researcher, reality is conceptualised as variables which are measured, and the primary objectives are to find how the variables are distributed, and especially how they are related to each other, and why. As is described in Chapter 2, a feature of the methodological history of quantitative social science has been the move away from the experimental method, where the researcher manipulates one or more variables in order to study their effects on other variables, to a broader non-experimental method and design, where the researcher uses naturally occurring variation in variables to study relationships between them. In other words, the strategy for studying the relationship between variables has broadened from a narrow concentration on experimental method to a more widely applicable approach using non-experimental methods.

The basic reason for this move has been the limited scope of the research questions which can be answered using the true experimental method, especially as social science areas expanded beyond psychology and education. For the great majority of research areas and topics, in a large number of social science areas, the researcher cannot manipulate variables for research purposes in order to study their effects. Research methodologists therefore developed non-experimental methods, by applying the logic of the experiment to the non-experimental research situation. This means that non-experimental quantitative methods are now an essential part of the methodological expertise of the social science researcher. It becomes correspondingly important for student researchers to learn these methods. The phrase 'non-experimental quantitative methods' really means quantitative survey methods which focus on the relationships between variables.

The purpose of this book is to teach these methods. To do that, it takes a simple model of the quantitative-survey-relating-variables, dismantles it to show how it works, and illustrates it with a detailed example. It then shows the flexibility of these methods, and how this model extends and generalises to more complex situations. I see mastery of this model, and of these methods, as an important objective in the training of social science researchers. In this, I agree with Babbie (1990: 40): 'If you fully understand the logic and skills of survey research, you will be excellently equipped to learn and to use other social research methods.'

Thus this book focuses on surveys which are:

- quantitative;
- concerned with relationships between variables.

Quantitative means that the survey is designed to produce numerical data, and proceeds by measuring variables. As noted, not all surveys are quantitative. But the focus here is on quantitative surveys which use numerical data produced by the measurement of variables.

Concerned with the relationship between variables means that the point of the survey is not simply to describe variables and how they are distributed. Its main aim is to study how variables are related to each other. This distinction is important, and the point is elaborated in Chapter 2.

In addition, the focus here is on surveys which are:

- small-scale;
- cross-sectional;
- based on the individual person as the unit of analysis;
- built around a self-administered questionnaire.

Small-scale means that I want to focus on situations where researchers have limited resources, and are therefore restricted in the size and scope of the survey they can conduct. A typical example of this is the dissertation or project of a student working in an area of social science.

Cross-sectional means that the survey collects data from people at one point in time, rather than at two or more points in time. This latter type of survey is longitudinal. While much of what is said here applies also to a longitudinal survey, the focus is on the cross-sectional survey since it is a more common method, especially for the graduate student.

The individual person as the unit of analysis means that the logic of the research is to investigate how individual people vary on the different variables, and how that individual-person-variance is related across the different variables. As noted later in this chapter (p. 5), surveys can be designed with other possible units of analysis (in educational research, for example, the school class, the school itself, or the school system could be the unit of analysis), but surveys with the individual as the unit of analysis are generally more common.

Built around the self-administered questionnaire is a simplification concerning the way the survey data are collected. Again, there are other possibilities, but the self-administered questionnaire (or paper-and-pencil self-report questionnaire, as it is sometimes called) is the most common method of data collection in the quantitative survey. This is elaborated in Chapters 3 and 4.[1]

The purpose of this book is therefore to describe the logic and strategy behind this type of survey, to analyse the different elements which make up this type of survey, to outline the steps by which such surveys are done, to demonstrate these steps through an example, and to show how the logic and strategy extend from simple to more complex investigations.

1.2   PLAN OF THE BOOK AND CHAPTER OUTLINE

The strategy for this book has two parts. The first part shows the central place of the quantitative survey in social research, identifies and analyses its elements, and shows how each element is operationalised (see Chapters 2–5). The second part of the strategy is to show how the simple model of the survey generalises to more complex versions (see Chapters 6 and 7).

The chapter plan follows this strategy. Thus, after this introductory chapter, Chapter 2 gives some methodological background to show the central place of the quantitative survey, Chapter 3 describes each of the main elements of the survey, and Chapter 4 shows how each element is operationalised through a set of steps. Chapter 5 then discusses the survey report and Chapter 6 contains the example, which is presented first in simple form and then extended. To finish the book, Chapter 7 shows how the logic of the simple model of the survey generalises to more complex examples.

The book concentrates initially on a simple model of the quantitative survey. It does this for ease of communication and to show both the logic of the quantitative survey and the steps involved in implementing that logic as clearly as possible. But later in the book, I show how the simplified version extends easily to more complex versions, and how the same logic supports the more complex versions. This means that the early chapters are written in simple independent–dependent variable terms, and the simple form of the example in Chapter 6 has two independent variables and one dependent variable. The more complex form of the example extends this, and the theme of extensions is taken further in Chapter 7.

A great strength of the quantitative survey, as a research strategy, is this breadth and flexibility. The type of quantitative survey described here is suitable for many different contexts, making it of great value in many different areas of social research. It is also easily adapted to different configurations of variables and different numbers of variables. This means that a wide variety of research problems can be investigated using these methods. Chapter 7 illustrates some of that variety.

1.3 IMPORTANT CONCEPTUAL TOOLS – INDEPENDENT AND DEPENDENT VARIABLES

As noted, the quantitative researcher sees the world as made up of variables, modelling what we do constantly in everyday life. Thus, in the physical world, we think in terms of such variables as length, mass or weight, temperature, and so on. In the economic world, we have such variables as inflation, unemployment and productivity, among many others. We can conceptualise aspects of the social world similarly. For example, people may differ in the variables age, gender, self-esteem, level of job satisfaction or motivation. Groups or organisations may differ in the variables size, cohesiveness, clarity of purpose or level of goal achievement.

We should notice two things about these commonplace examples of thinking in terms of variables. Both have important technical consequences. First, a variable is seen as the property (or characteristic) of some entity. Most often, in social research, the entity is the individual person – it is the individual's gender or level of self-esteem or motivation which is of interest. But the entity can also be the family, the group, the organisation, the city, the industry or the economy. This is the technical issue of the 'unit of analysis', something we need to get clear when planning a survey. For simplicity this book describes surveys where the individual person is the unit of analysis. But the logic and methods described are the same for other possible units of analysis. Secondly, the property – the variable – may vary either in categories or along a continuum. Thus gender varies in categories (male or female), whereas job satisfaction ranges along a continuum from low to high. This is the important technical issue of categorical versus continuous variables, discussed in detail in Chapter 4 (pp. 55–6). This is a crucial distinction with a variety of implications and it needs to be clearly understood.

As also noted, the quantitative researcher is centrally interested in the relationships between the variables, rather than in just describing the variables. Typically, each variable has a particular conceptual status in the researcher's thinking. This means that the researcher has a *conceptual framework* for thinking about the variables. Indeed, a characteristic of a good quantitative survey is that its conceptual framework can be clearly described. As is shown in Chapter 3, getting the conceptual framework clear is part of the planning of the quantitative survey. The most common conceptual framework in our everyday thinking is a causal one. We think almost automatically of possible causal relationships among variables. In the simplest two-variable case, one is the 'cause' and the other is the 'effect'. We need to adapt this sort of thinking and language to the research context.

In view of philosophical problems with the concept of causation, it is customary in empirical research to use the terms 'independent' and 'dependent' variables in place of the terms 'cause' and 'effect'. In doing so, our thinking – our conceptualising and theorising and our view of the 'direction of influence' between the variables (Rosenberg, 1968) – has not changed, but we have tidied up our use of language. Thus, for practical purposes, independent variable effectively means cause, and dependent variable effectively means effect. The simplest example of this is two variables, one the independent variable (cause) and the other the dependent variable (effect). The conceptual framework for this is:

Independent variable ———————▶ Dependent variable
           (IV)   (DV)

Examples of this, expressed as research questions, are:

- What is the relationship between motivation (IV) and achievement (DV) among secondary school students?
- What is the relationship between salary (IV) and job satisfaction (DV) in different occupations?
- What is the relationship between gender (IV) and occupational aspiration (DV) among university students?

While there are many possible extensions of this simple framework, one of the most common and most useful is several independent variables and one dependent variable.

This reflects the more realistic idea of multiple causation, and is dealt with in detail in Chapter 7 when the simple model of the quantitative survey is generalised to more complex models. The conceptual framework in this case is:

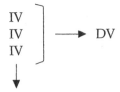

Examples are:

- What is the relationship between intelligence, social status and motivation (IVs) and achievement in secondary school (DV)?

- What is the relationship between marital status, employment status, income, gender and body mass index (IVs) and depression (DV)? (Allison, 1999)
- What is the relationship between age, income, family size and fatalism (IVs) and vitamin use (DV)? (Burns and Bush, 1995)

Clearly, the conceptual framework for thinking about and ordering the variables is an important part of the type of quantitative survey in focus here. It is only when the researcher has got the conceptual framework clear that the planning for the survey can move from the conceptual to the operational level.

1.4 MODEL OF RESEARCH

This book is based on a general model of empirical research which is suitable for both quantitative and qualitative studies. I see such research as an organised, systematic and logical process of inquiry, using empirical information to answer questions or test hypotheses. Sometimes the information will be quantitative, sometimes qualitative, and sometimes a mixture of the two. Whatever the case, similar processes and logic underlie both the inquiry and the way in which evidence is used to answer research questions and reach conclusions. As already noted, this book on surveys deals only with quantitative data.

This view of research, which I use as a teaching device, is shown in diagram form in Figure 1.1 below. It stresses the central role of research questions and has four main features:

- framing the research in terms of research questions;
- determining what data are necessary to answer those questions;
- designing research to collect and analyse those data;
- using the data to answer the questions.

Importantly, in this view, research begins with substantive issues – what are we trying to find out here? – before moving on to methodological issues – how will we do this? Questions come before methods, and what methods we use should be governed by what we are trying to find out. If our questions are about the relationships between variables, and if the situation is non-experimental – that is, if it does not involve the researcher artificially manipulating variables for research purposes – then we have exactly the sort of quantitative-survey-relating-variables described earlier. The implication of this is that the proper starting point for the survey is the matter of objectives and research questions. This is described and illustrated in Chapters 3 and 4.

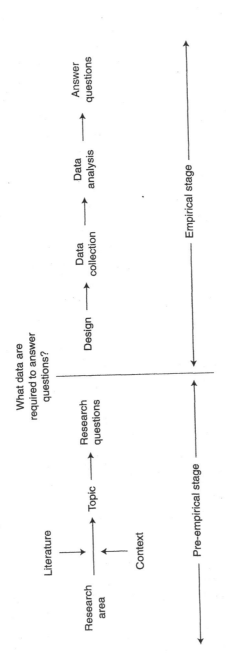

FIGURE 1.1 *Simplified model of research*

A second implication is that the type of survey described in this book is an example of a prespecified or prestructured research design. Looking across present-day social research, *Introduction to Social Research* (Punch, 1998: 23–7) presented a continuum of research designs concerned with the timing of structure in the design. At end points of the continuum, it drew the contrast between prespecified or prestructured designs (with clear research questions, tight designs and prestructured data) and unfolding designs (with general guiding questions, loose designs and data not prestructured). Quantitative-surveys-relating-variables are a clear example of prestructured research designs. This means that careful planning of each step is an important characteristic and an essential ingredient of the quantitative survey, and for dissertation students there are important benefits to presenting a detailed description of the plan for the survey in your research proposal. The planning needs to be based on an understanding of each main element of the survey and of how the elements fit together. The elements are described in Chapter 3, operationalised in Chapter 4 and illustrated in Chapter 6. Before that, however, Chapter 2 gives necessary background to understanding the important place of the quantitative survey in social research.

1.5 REVIEW CONCEPTS

quantitative survey
quantitative-survey-relating-variables
cross-sectional survey – longitudinal survey
unit of analysis
self-administered questionnaire – self-report questionnaire

variables
continuous variables
categorical variables
independent variables
dependent variables

conceptual framework
model of research

NOTE

1. Not all quantitative-surveys-relating-variables are based on a self-administered, self-report questionnaire. For example, a traffic survey

may be based on structured observation leading to quantitative data. Or a survey may require the observational rating of the incidence and extent of violence in a school playground and then relate these measures to other variables.

2

Relationships between Variables

CONTENTS

Chapter 1 argued for the central importance of the quantitative-survey-relating-variables in social science research and therefore its central role in research training. This chapter gives methodological and substantive background to the reasons for this importance. It then discusses relationships between variables, explains the focus on small-scale studies, describes the basic strategy of the quantitative survey, identifies its elements, and points out some of its limitations.

2.1 BACKGROUND

The reasons for the central position of the quantitative survey as a research strategy are both methodological and substantive.

[a] Methodological

The essence of quantitative research is the study of the relationships between variables. For the quantitative researcher, reality is conceptualised as variables, and the ultimate objective is to find out how different variables are related to each other, and why. Historically, there have been two main strategies for doing that.

The first is the experimental method and design where the researcher manipulates one or more variables in order to study the effects on other variables. A simple educational research example with one independent variable and one dependent variable is: One group of students is taught a particular subject by method A, and an equivalent group is taught the same subject by method B. We want to know which group does best on a test of learning. The independent variable is teaching method; the dependent variable is learning. We manipulate the independent variable in the research in order to study its effects on the dependent variable.

The second is non-experimental method and design where the researcher uses naturally occurring variation in variables to study the relationship between them. 'Naturally occurring variation' means that the variable is not artificially manipulated for purposes of the research. The above example can be rephrased to fit this description in these terms: It happens that one group of students is being taught the subject by method A, and another group is being taught the same subject by method B. Using the same measure of learning, the researcher looks for differences between the two groups in their test scores, with a view to attributing these differences in learning to differences in the teaching method. As before, teaching method is the independent variable and learning is the dependent variable.

The logic of these two main approaches is described more fully in *Introduction to Social Research* (Punch, 1998: 71–81) – the above summary shows only the bare bones of the matter. In particular, this summary does not mention the need for the control of other variables. To show that differences in learning are due to teaching method we would need to show that they are not due to other things – we need to control other variables. The experiment does that physically in the way it is designed. The non-experiment does that statistically in the way it analyses data.

In the historical development of some of the social sciences, the experimental method was originally seen as the main research strategy, and is still used extensively in certain social science areas (for example, psychology, educational psychology). There is good reason for this – it was modelled on the methods used in other sciences, especially physics, chemistry and agriculture, and it was seen as the surest basis for establishing the all-important cause–effect relationships between variables. As social science has broadened, however, non-experimental methods have become increasingly important, and non-experimental methodology has developed accordingly, especially in techniques for the statistical control of variables. As noted in Chapter 1, the main reason for this has been the limited scope of the research questions which can be answered using the experimental method, together with increased awareness of the ethical issues involved in experimentation. In other words, for the great majority of research areas and topics, in the majority of social science research areas, the researcher cannot experimentally manipulate variables for research purposes in order to study their effects. It was therefore necessary to develop non-experimental equivalents of, or approximations to, experimental design. This was done by applying the logic of experimental design to the non-experimental research situation.[1]

This means that non-experimental research methods are now an essential part of the methodological expertise of the social science researcher. It becomes correspondingly important for student researchers to learn these methods. The quantitative-survey-relating-variables, as described in this book, is the foundation of these non-experimental research methods. Such surveys can range from simple to complex, in the number of variables they use and in the conceptual frameworks for organising them. But simple and complex surveys both use the same logic and the same basic strategy. Because of that, I believe that the best order of teaching and learning is to begin with the simple model of the survey and to work up to more complex models, as is done in this book.

I believe also that it is timely to reassert the importance of the quantitative survey as a basic strategy in research training. With the massive swing towards qualitative methods of the last 25 or so years, there is a danger that such a central tool can be overlooked or downgraded in the way new generations of social science researchers are trained.

[b] Substantive

Here I take a perspective from sociology to see why, from a substantive point of view, the quantitative-survey-relating-variables is so important in social science research. It is appropriate to look to sociology because it is one of the basic social science disciplines and its perspectives pervade many of the more applied social science areas.

In the tradition established by Samuel Stouffer (Stouffer et al., 1949) and extended by Paul Lazarsfeld, Patricia Kendall and Robert Merton (Kendall and Lazarsfeld, 1950; Merton and Lazarsfeld 1950), Morris Rosenberg made important contributions to quantitative empirical work in sociology. It is his perspective that I will use here. In his words:

- 'The sociologist is characteristically interested in the relationship of *social experience* to *individual mental processes and acts*' (Rosenberg, 1968: 23, my emphasis); and again

- 'The relationship between a *property* and a *disposition* or *act* is probably the central type of relationship in social research' (Rosenberg, 1968: 17, my emphasis).

Let us analyse in some detail what this means. 'Social experience', as used in the first quotation above, refers to the idea that different social experiences are typically associated with membership in different social categories. We are all members of different social categories – for example gender categories (male or female), country of birth categories (England, Australia, India, etc.), social class categories (lower, middle, upper), religious affiliation categories (Muslim, Christian, Jew, Hindu, no religion, etc.), and so on.

Rosenberg's point is that membership of such social categories typically brings with it different types of social experience. Two examples are:

- boys and girls may have different types of experience in the school system by virtue of their gender 'category membership' or gender group;
- older people are likely to have quite different educational backgrounds and experiences from younger people, by virtue of their age group.

'Membership of social category' can also be thought of as a 'property', as used in the second Rosenberg quotation given above. That is, we can think of gender or country of birth or age or social class as social properties which a particular person possesses. 'Individual mental processes or acts', in the first quotation, or 'dispositions and acts', in the second, mean the things that we, as individuals, feel (dispositions) and do (acts).

So what Rosenberg is saying can be represented as a diagram:

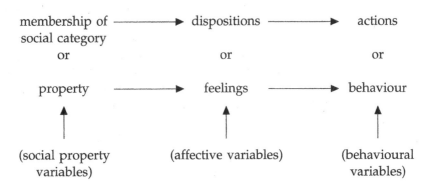

What Rosenberg calls dispositions, and what I have called feelings, are often more generally described as affective variables. This term includes feelings, attitudes, opinions, values, perceptions, and so on. Thus, a more general statement of Rosenberg's idea is:

Social properties ⎯⎯▶ affective variables ⎯⎯▶ behavioural variables[2]

The general research question implied here is: What is the relationship between social properties, affective variables and behavioural variables?

There are many examples of this kind of thinking because it is so common. Here are two examples, phrased as questions:

- What are the differences between girls and boys (social property) in their attitudes towards secondary school (affective variable), and in their secondary school subject choices (behavioural variable)?
- What are the differences between older and younger workers (social property) in their preferred working environments (affective variable) and their rate of absenteeism (behavioural variable)?

How do social researchers investigate such clearly empirical questions? The strategy for answering them is quite straightforward. To take the first question above, we study a sample of boys and girls, we work out what data we will take to represent their attitudes towards school and their actions with respect to subject choices, we collect such data, and we analyse the data to see if there are systematic differences between boys and girls. To take the second question, we take a sample of older and younger workers, we collect data about their preferred working environments and their rates of absenteeism, and we analyse the data to see if there are systematic differences between the two groups of workers on these variables.

These descriptions of the strategy follow exactly the logic of the quantitative survey, which is described in general terms in section 2.4 (pp. 22–3) of this chapter. In other words, Rosenberg's perspective points directly to the quantitative survey as the research strategy to investigate the questions it raises.

The framework that Rosenberg's perspective provides is important and useful to us for several reasons:

- It provides a ready-made general conceptual framework for us. We can either use the framework as is, or modify it to represent our thinking about the variables we are studying (for example, see note 2 at the end of this chapter).

- It is an organising framework. It helps us both to conceptualise and to order our thoughts about the sorts of question we may want to investigate in research.
- It is applicable across a wide range of situations. It is relevant to so many situations and questions of interest that it may well be a typical way of thinking. Certainly it is very common.
- Its emphasis on social properties reflects a major organising principle of social life. In that sense, it is realistic.
- It is flexible and easily capable of extensions and modifications. In other words it is versatile.
- By identifying conceptually abstract variables (properties, dispositions and actions) it encourages us to think of other specific examples of these for investigation. We can easily think of additional properties, dispositions and actions which it would be interesting and useful to investigate.

For both methodological and substantive reasons, therefore, the quantitative-survey-relating-variables emerges as a central research strategy. Let us now turn to the emphasis on relating variables in the quantitative survey.

2.2 RELATIONSHIPS BETWEEN VARIABLES

Why do I keep stressing relationships between variables? One reason is because the concept of the relationship between variables is at the heart of quantitative research. In a fundamental sense, quantitative research is essentially about investigating and understanding how and why variables are related to each other. The other reason is that I believe that quantitative surveys, especially when they are academic projects and dissertations, are better when they have this focus.

Given that quantitative research is centrally interested in how variables are related to each other, there are three main general questions leading to three main types of study in quantitative research, as shown in Table 2.1.

TABLE 2.1 *Research questions and types of research*

General question	Type of research
How are the variables distributed?	Descriptive
How are the variables related?	Descriptive–explanatory
Why are the variables distributed and related this way?	Explanatory

It is the distinction between the first two questions in this table, the questions of distribution and relationship, that I want to focus on now.

[a] Distribution of variables

Referring back to Rosenberg's framework of properties, dispositions and actions:

- the distribution of a social property variable shows how many people fall into the different categories of the variable;
- the distribution of a disposition or affective variable shows how many people think about or feel or see things in a certain way;
- the distribution of an action or behavioural variable shows how many people act (or intend to act) in a certain way.

These distributions are usually expressed as proportions or percentages. Some examples of distribution statements are:

For the variable gender
- 43% of respondents were male
- 57% of respondents were female

For the variable age
- 29% of respondents were 25 years or younger
- 34% of respondents were between 26 and 45 years
- 37% of respondents were 46 years or older

For the variable attitude towards supervisor
- 20% of respondents reported a favourable attitude
- 50% of respondents reported a neutral attitude
- 30% of respondents reported an unfavourable attitude

Surveys are carried out to produce such statements as these, which are prominent in such areas as:

- political polling – how many voters think or feel this or that?
- market research – how many consumers like or dislike this brand, image or product?
- change research – how many people support or oppose a proposed change?

Surveys to produce these distribution statements are sometimes called 'status' surveys, or 'normative' surveys. Clearly, these are purely descriptive statements, producing only a first level of knowledge.

Status or normative surveys are usually not seen as sufficient, in themselves, for research projects in the academic context – especially not in the post-graduate research context. They are seen as too descriptive, producing knowledge which is too low-level and weak in the sense of being 'time bound' and easily changeable. Thus, for example, 65% of people may say they support a particular change now, but how do we know what that figure will be at some other time, even soon after? Descriptive statements about how variables are distributed are normally the first step in a study of relationships between the variables, as is shown in the example in Chapter 6, but they are only a first step. Asking only descriptive questions of the data in a quantitative survey is usually a lost opportunity – most such studies could easily go further and investigate relationships between variables.

[b] Relationships between variables

To ask about relationships between variables is to ask about the extent to which, and the ways in which, two (or more) variables vary together, or co-vary. Such questions can apply to any number of variables. Here I restrict the discussion to the simplest two-variable case.

Examples of questions about the relationship between two variables are:

- What is the relationship between ethnicity and crime?
- What is the relationship between age and TV watching?
- What is the relationship between religiosity and prejudice?
- What is the relationship between length of employment and job satisfaction?
  (Babbie, 1990; Alreck and Settle, 1995; Allison, 1999)

In one sense, statements relating variables are descriptive. They describe the way two variables relate to each other. Sometimes this is stated as differences between groups, an alternative expression of relationships between variables which is discussed later in this section. In another sense, such statements are partly explanatory, or a step on the way to explanation. That is why they are shown as descriptive–explanatory in Table 2.1. Certainly, they are more powerful statements than the earlier distribution statements. They are a 'step on the way to explanation' in two senses, one methodological, one substantive:

- Methodologically, the key concept here is the variance of a variable, and how we can account for that variance. We understand and can 'explain' a variable when we can account for all or most of its variance. We account for its variance by finding how it relates to other variables – that is, by knowing what variance it holds in common with other variables. This idea is described in more detail in Chapter 7.

- Substantively, statements of relationships between variables lead us, almost naturally, to questions of why and how that relationship comes about, and how it might vary in different contexts. A typical and useful next step here is to ask about how the relationship is affected by other variables.

Continuous and categorical variables

Chapter 1 mentioned the distinction between continuous and categorical variables, and the discussion so far about relationships between variables has been mostly in terms of continuous variables. There is an important clarification to add for the case of categorical variables. One way of asking whether two variables are related, when one of them is categorical, is to ask whether there are differences between the groups (formed by the categorical variable) on the other variable.

Consider the following pairs of questions:

What is the relationship between gender and attitude to school? (relationship between variables)
Do boys and girls differ in their attitude to school? (difference between groups)

And again:

What is the relationship between employment type (government, corporate, self-employed) and job satisfaction? (relationship between variables)
Are there differences in job satisfaction between people who work in government organisations, private corporations or are self-employed? (difference between groups)

Within each pair, the questions are logically equivalent. They mean the same thing or, more accurately, the 'difference-between-groups' version of the question is more specific than the 'relationships-between-variables' version. Thus, in the first example above, to say that gender is related to attitude to school is to say that boys and girls differ in their attitude to school. In the second example, to say that employment type is

---

Box 2.1   Relationships between variables ◄──► Differences between groups

When one variable is categorical and another continuous, the two variables are related if there is a difference on the continuous variable between the categories (or groups). This applies whether the categorical variable has two categories (dichotomous) or more than two categories.

Examples

Categorical variable	Continuous variable
Gender	Self-esteem
(boys, girls)	

- Is gender related to self-esteem?
- Do boys and girls differ in self-esteem?

Type of school attended	Secondary school
(Government, independent	achievement
non-Catholic, independent	
Catholic)	

- Is the type of school attended related to secondary school achievement?
- Do students from Government, independent non-Catholic and independent Catholic schools differ in their achievement?

Country of birth	Political orientation
(UK, Australia, India, China)	

- Is country of birth related to political orientation?
- Are there differences in political orientation between people born in UK, Australia, India, China?

---

related to job satisfaction is to say that government employees, corporate employees and self-employed people differ in their level of job satisfaction. The logical equivalence of the two types of question (and corresponding statement) is illustrated in Box 2.1. Since the first way of asking the question is more general, including the second way as a special case when one of the variables is categorical, I will use the first way, and talk mostly about relationships between variables. Sometimes, however, this means differences between groups.

Survey projects which study the relationship between variables are generally more acceptable in academic work than those which study only the distribution of variables, for several interrelated reasons:

- They are more powerful. When we know how variables are related to each other, we know much more than just how they are distributed. Indeed, the way we account for the distribution of a variable is to study its relationships with other variables.
- Knowing the relationship between variables enables prediction. If we know how two variables are related, we can predict scores on one variable from the other variable. Chapter 7 shows the importance of the concept of prediction. On a more philosophical level, prediction and explanation are two sides of the same coin. A major test of the validity of an explanation is its ability to predict.
- As noted, they are a step on the way to explanation. In this sense, they are much more interesting and provocative. They lead naturally to the central explanatory question: Why? Why are these variables related in this way? How does it come about? What can be going on to produce these relationships? This in turn opens up both ideas of social processes (which are often then investigated qualitatively) and the role of still other variables in understanding the two-variable relationship. Indeed, one of the main ways we understand a two-variable relationship is by introducing a third variable into the analysis and studying what happens to the original relationship (see Rosenberg, 1968). This is an important point of general research strategy. Focusing first on the relationships between variables, and then on explaining that relationship, is an excellent and general theory-building strategy for quantitative research. As researchers, we should always ask how and why variables are related. This is in line with the overriding aim of research – to explain – and opens up leads for further research.
- In another sense, they lead to research which is theory oriented. This is especially the case when we frame hypotheses about relationships, and are forced to consider the possible role of other variables.

In summary, relationships between variables are at the heart of quantitative research, and of the type of quantitative survey considered here. If you are a project or dissertation student, I recommend you try to ensure that your survey focuses on relationships between variables, using the distribution of your variables as a first step. It will help to organise your thinking if you use the property–disposition–action framework of Rosenberg, and the general questions shown in Table 2.1. In particular, it will help to extend your questions from distribution ones to relationship ones.

2.3 SMALL-SCALE SURVEYS

There are three reasons why I concentrate in this book on small-scale surveys.

The first is the value of the small-scale survey as a vehicle for learning about quantitative empirical research in the social sciences. I have argued that the quantitative-survey-relating-variables is a central strategy in quantitative research. It follows that understanding and learning how to execute the quantitative survey should be a central part of research training. As a pedagogical strategy, a good way to do this is to study a small-scale model, and to work through a small-scale example in all its stages. Then the model and example can be extended and generalised.

The second reason is that I believe that the substantive contribution of small-scale surveys is often downgraded or overlooked in the way knowledge develops. Research-based knowledge in any field builds and accumulates as much through the weight of evidence, where the results of numerous smaller studies are accumulated, as through the findings of a single definitive study. Thus well-conducted small-scale surveys have a valuable contribution to make. Of course, due weight needs to be given to the limitations or biases in any particular sample used in small-scale surveys, and the researcher has constantly to keep the question of generalisability in view. Nor, of course, do I have anything against the single, definitive large-scale study. But the point often overlooked is that small-scale surveys, competently and carefully executed, can make valuable substantive contributions.

The third reason is that a deliberate focus of this book is the work of research students in different social science areas. There are many excellent and comprehensive books on survey research in social science, but they are very often 'ideal-type' in the sense that they describe good practice under assumptions of substantial (or unlimited) resources. The graduate student, invariably limited in time and other resources, and often working alone, is, in my experience, frequently daunted by this literature. This book is therefore directed at the small-scale survey researcher. It deals directly with the conception, planning, design, execution and reporting of small-scale surveys, such as those often done in graduate student dissertations and other small-scale research projects. Such projects can have both important learning benefits and important contribution-to-knowledge benefits.

2.4 THE QUANTITATIVE SURVEY STRATEGY

A quantitative-survey-relating-variables begins with its objectives and research questions. These define the variables of interest in the study.

Assuming, as earlier, the individual person is the unit of analysis, the essential idea of the quantitative survey is then to measure a group of people on the variables of interest and to see how those variables are related to each other across the sample studied. Putting that idea into practice requires four main decisions:

- We must decide what the purposes or objectives are and what we are trying to find out in the survey. This is the job of developing objectives and research questions. Once they are specific enough, they will tell us what the variables of interest are and what data we need to answer the questions.
- We must then decide how the variables will be measured and how the data will be collected – what data collection questions will we ask and how will we ask them? As noted in Chapter 1, I make the assumption here that the self-administered questionnaire will be the general method of data collection.
- We must decide from whom the data will be collected – that is, we must select a sample for the study.
- We must decide how to analyse the data in order to answer the questions.

These decisions point to the key elements of the survey, listed in section 2.5 below and discussed in Chapters 3 and 4.

There needs to be an internal coherence and consistent logic running through our decisions on these matters. The different parts of our survey project should 'hang together'. A technical term for this is the internal validity of our survey research design, a term originally used in experimental design. Unlike experimental methods, the strategy for the quantitative survey does not involve the manipulation of variables or the imposition of treatments for research purposes. The survey researcher studies the world 'as it is'. But the concept of internal validity is just as important.

2.5 THE ELEMENTS OF THE QUANTITATIVE SURVEY

Following the above description of the survey strategy, there are six main elements in a quantitative survey, shown below. To these six I have added a seventh, the survey report. The elements are:

- the objectives;
- the research questions;

- the questionnaire;
- the sample;
- the data collection strategy;
- the data analysis strategy;
- the report.

These are the topics for the next three chapters. The first of these, Chapter 3, describes each of these elements. Chapter 4 then shows the steps involved in implementing each of them, combining them into a survey project. Chapter 5 discusses and describes the survey research report.

2.6 REVIEW CONCEPTS

social property variables
affective variables (dispositions)
behavioural variables (actions)
distribution of variables
relationships between variables
status surveys – normative surveys
continuous variables – relationships between variables

↕   ↕

categorical variables – differences between groups
quantitative survey strategy
quantitative survey elements

NOTES

1. I do not mean to imply that early social science research used only experimental design. There were always surveys, even in psychology. The point that I am stressing is the rapid advance in quantitative survey methodology as limitations of the experimental method became clear.

2. We can conceptualise and illustrate this relationship slightly differently, as shown below:

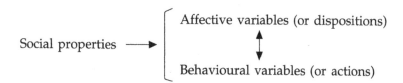

This alternative conceptual framework implies different ideas about how category membership, dispositions and actions are related to each other. It also implies different research questions, and different methods in the analysis of our survey data.

3

Elements of the Survey: Description

CONTENTS

This chapter describes six of the main elements in a quantitative survey. The seventh, the survey report, is described separately in Chapter 5. The aim of this chapter is to develop an understanding of what each element is, the role it plays in the survey, and the issues it raises. Therefore this chapter is discursive and descriptive. It leads into Chapter 4, which is more hands-on and presents the concrete steps for implementing each element of the survey. A theme throughout these two chapters is the need to plan carefully and to anticipate issues which will arise, rather than dealing with them *ad hoc*, or as an afterthought, as the survey proceeds.

3.1 SURVEY OBJECTIVES

It seems self-evident to say that the survey researcher needs to know, and communicate clearly, the objectives of the survey. But it is not always well understood that identifying, clarifying and precisely stating survey objectives takes time and effort, that this effort is a good invest-ment, and that there is an important connection between survey objectives and research questions, and through research questions to everything that follows in the survey. Experienced researchers know also that the first statement of the objectives and research questions for the quantitative survey is rarely the final one. Developing the objectives and research questions, and especially achieving a precise statement of them, is usually an iterative process, one of 'successive approximations' and one that takes time.

What are survey objectives? They are a statement, at a reasonably high level of generality and abstraction, of what the survey is trying to find out. They are the overall purposes or aims of the inquiry. They may be encapsulated in one statement, or they may require several statements. Here are some examples of survey objectives:

- To investigate the relationship between mental ability and time on task as independent variables and school achievement as dependent variable (Chapter 6).
- To investigate the relationship between mental ability and time on task as independent variables and school achievement as dependent variable, after controlling for alienation and in the context of differ-ent social class levels (Chapter 6).
- To investigate staff perceptions of the effectiveness of a programme of training, and to examine the differences in perceived effectiveness between different staff groups.

3.2 RESEARCH QUESTIONS

The research questions take the generalised statement of objectives and make them more specific and concrete. They begin the process of connecting abstract concepts, as used in the statement of objectives, to the empirical world of specific and concrete data and data indicators, as used in the actual research. The clarification of research questions is just as important as the clarification of objectives.

A central feature of empirical research, which applies very much to the quantitative-survey-relating-variables, is that data exist and are collected at a very specific or concrete level, but that the purpose or objective of the research is to reach conclusions and make statements at a much higher level of generality or abstraction. This means that there are specific pieces of data at the lowest level, abstract concepts at the highest level, and a gap between these levels. Disciplined research requires that we establish logical connections between these levels. Often this is best done by having more than one intermediate or connecting level between these

Box 3.1 Hierarchy of concepts

More general

Hierarchy	Example (from Chapter 6)
Research area	Students' achievement at school
Research topic	Determinants of scholastic achievement
Objectives	To investigate relationships between mental ability, time on task and school achievement
General research question	What is the relationship between mental ability and time on task as independent variables and school achievement as dependent variable?
Specific research questions	What is the relationship between mental ability and school achievement? What is the relationship between time on task and school achievement? What is the relationship between mental ability and time on task? What is the joint relationship between mental ability, time on task and school achievement?
Data collection questions	The specific items and questions used to collect the data for the variables mental ability, time on task and school achievement

More specific

levels. This leads to a hierarchy of levels of generality and abstraction, which was described in *Developing Effective Research Proposals* (Punch, 2000: 21–7), and which is shown in Box 3.1.

In designing, and later in conducting and reporting our research, we need to move up and down across these levels of generality or abstraction. This means that we need to have logical links across the different levels. In planning research, the hierarchy shown in Box 3.1 can be very useful. As a type of research, the quantitative survey fits nicely into this hierarchy, as shown by the example in the box, which is taken from Chapter 6. There is no need to be obsessive in the way we use the hierarchy, but it can help in making our thinking orderly and systematic.

In particular, framing research questions first in general terms, then in specific terms, and then using the empirical criterion to identify the data indicators, helps build the tight logical links needed between abstract concepts and empirical data indicators. The last distinction in the hierarchy, between specific research questions and data collection questions, is important, and brings us to the empirical criterion, discussed below.

Moving up and down across this hierarchy of levels of abstraction is not some mysterious process used only in the esoteric world of research. On the contrary, it is a commonplace activity, done constantly and unproblematically in our thinking and talking about everyday things. The difference in the 'esoteric world of research' is that the links between these levels need to be systematic, organised, logical, demonstrable and communicable. Interestingly, this point applies just as much to certain types of qualitative research as it does to quantitative research.[1]

A good way of using this hierarchy is to move down from area to topic to objectives, and then on to research questions, first general and then specific. This splits the process into a number of steps and is a strategy that works in many research situations. It is especially useful for the type of quantitative survey we are discussing here.

General and specific research questions, arranged this way, have these important functions:

- they organise the project and give it direction and coherence;
- they delimit the project, showing its boundaries;
- they keep the researcher focused during the project;
- they provide a framework for writing up the project;
- they point to the data that will be needed in the project – in particular, they connect the empirical operations, at the level of concrete data and data indicators, to the more abstract concepts. This means that they guide both the data collection (what data are needed to answer these questions – see empirical criterion below) and the data analysis (how will the data be analysed to answer the questions – see section 3.6, pp. 44–5).

The empirical criterion for research questions

It should be clear, in well-stated research questions, what data are required to answer them. Indeed, if it is not clear, the researcher has more work to do in developing the questions. An important check, as each research question is being framed, is to ask what data will be needed to answer it. When that is clear for each research question, the researcher is ready to move to data collection questions. In the quantitative survey, the data collection questions operationalise the variables and together constitute the survey questionnaire.

Conceptual framework

Conceptual frameworks were discussed in Chapter 1, and it was pointed out that independent–dependent variable set-ups were the most common. The conceptual framework is important in developing, and later in writing about, the quantitative survey. Indeed, some would say that it should be a requirement of this kind of survey that the researcher be able to sketch the conceptual framework before the study proceeds. Once again, if that cannot be done, it probably means that more work is required. The conceptual framework is developed alongside the research questions and needs to be consistent with them. Examples are shown in Chapter 4 (p. 52) and Chapter 6 (pp. 82, 92).

When the general and specific research questions are fixed, and when each specific question meets the empirical criterion, the research planning can move to the data collection questions, which will be brought together in the survey questionnaire.

3.3 THE QUESTIONNAIRE

The survey questionnaire[2] is guided by the research questions and is the data collection tool. Therefore it sits between the research questions and the strategy and process of data collection. It is discussed in this chapter under six headings:

- its relationship to the research questions;
- definitions of variables;
- where the questionnaire comes from;
- multiple-item scales;
- the role of pilot testing;
- the constraints within which the questionnaire is developed.

Relationship to research questions

Once the research questions conform to the empirical criterion, they tell us what data are needed in the survey. They also provide a map for the questionnaire. Thus the starting point for the questionnaire is the research questions. Together they give a list of the variables which will need to be measured in the questionnaire, and any other information required. As is described in the next chapter, the first step in organising the questionnaire is therefore to go back over the research questions and list the variables for which data will be required. The data collection questions for each variable will then represent the operational definition of that variable.

Definitions of variables

The research questions together give a list of the variables the survey questionnaire will need to measure. It is logical at this point to define the variables. Definitions of variables exist at two levels – the conceptual level and the operational level. As noted, the data collection questions for each variable together represent the operational definition of that variable. Above that sits the conceptual definition, where the variable is defined in more abstract terms. Thus the conceptual definition of time on task is the amount of out-of-class time a student spends studying. The operational definition is given by the 12 items used to collect data about the time students spend studying (see Chapter 6, p. 84). Again, a conceptual definition of leadership behaviour is given in two main dimensions:

- Structure reflects the extent to which an individual is likely to define and structure his or her own role and those of subordinates towards goal attainment.
- Consideration reflects the extent to which an individual is likely to have job relationships characterised by mutual trust, respect of their feelings.

The operational definition of these two dimensions is given by the 40 items of the Leader Behaviour Description Questionnaire (see Miller, 1991: 441).

Where the questionnaire comes from

The main issue here is whether the researcher will develop a question-naire, in its entirety, specifically for this survey, whether some already existing survey instrument can be used, or whether some combination of these two alternatives is best. Four points are relevant to this issue.

First, much survey research has already been done, in many countries. Therefore many excellent survey questionnaires already exist. A major problem, however, is locating these already existing questionnaires and measuring instruments. Some collections of them do exist,[3] and regular reading of the appropriate journals and research reports will give leads to other instruments. A serious survey researcher builds a collection of these instruments across time from such reading. But for the graduate student, locating existing questionnaires can be challenging.

Secondly, it is necessary to assess the quality of a questionnaire once it is located: Is this a good questionnaire, or not? This raises the important issue of the quality of data, discussed in section 3.5 (pp. 41–2). Some key concepts for considering the quality of the data are given there.

Thirdly, how much measurement expertise and knowledge does the researcher have or have ready access to? Constructing good measuring instruments is not easy, and measurement itself is a specialised field with its theories, models and technical literature. On the other hand, very effective measures can be constructed by researchers who have the necessary measurement expertise. Much depends here on whether the survey is concerned with what we might call major variables, involving multiple-item scales, or not. This point is elaborated in Box 3.2.

Fourthly, the second and third points above interact, with obvious implications. If the researcher has little or no measurement expertise, the attempt to construct measures, especially if major variables and multiple-item scales are involved, is not realistic and fraught with difficulty, with unfortunate consequences for the quality of the data. Each situation is different, but as a general rule I would recommend these guidelines for the question of whether or not to develop a new instrument for your survey.

Where possible, prefer the use of already existing instruments, in whole or in part, to developing your own. If you are working with established major variables, this is definitely the case. Remember that you can use part of an existing questionnaire. Remember also that any use of an existing questionnaire may involve copyright clearance, and that it is often necessary to adapt the wording of an existing questionnaire to 'local' conditions. This is not always straightforward – for example, there are special considerations and problems in cross-cultural research, which often involve the translation of survey questions across languages. Often successful surveys finish up with questionnaires which are a mixture of existing instruments, perhaps modified, and specifically developed parts, scales or items.

Multiple-item scales

Some variables are measured by a single item or indicator. They may be categorical variables, such as gender or country of birth, where one clearly worded item will suffice. Or they may be continuous variables –

Box 3.2 Major variables

By major variables (or complex concepts – Sapsford, 1999) I mean variables that are seen as centrally important in a field of research. Much empirical research has already been done with them and instruments and scales therefore already exist to measure them. They are usually multi-dimensional variables and multiple-item scales are usually involved.

Examples of major variables from different social research areas

Psychology	Education	Management
Mental ability	Achievement	Leader behaviour
Personality	Motivation	Decision-making
Self-esteem	Alienation	style
Locus of control	Learning preference	Communication
	styles	patterns
		Job satisfaction

Organisational Studies	Sociology	Family Studies
Organisational	Occupational	Child-rearing
structure	prestige	practices
Organisational climate	Quality of life	Family closeness
Morale	Values	Marital satisfaction
Group cohesiveness	Social participation	Parental involvement

---

something is being rated on a scale, for example – where the interest is in responses to the individual item itself. But for other variables, and especially for major variables, we are more likely to measure using a scale score made up from responses to multiple items.

In this case, our interest is not so much in responses to individual items. Rather, the individual item is an indicator of the deeper-level trait or characteristic being measured. A scale score for the variable will be formed by aggregating the responses to a number of individual items. This is a multiple-item scale and special considerations now arise. Specifically, dimensionality and internal consistency are now involved and, in good quality research, need to be demonstrated rather than simply assumed (or, even worse, ignored). Established instruments will have taken this into account, and well-known ones will have published such information. If you are developing a multiple-item scale for one or more of your variables, you will have to take this issue into account. This is an example of the need for measurement expertise in questionnaire construction, and numerous writers provide guidance here – see, for example, Babbie (1990), Oppenheim (1992), Alreck and Settle (1995), Sapsford, (1999), and see also Appendix 1. In addition, Tuckman (1999: 216–20) provides a clear example of the steps involved in developing a multiple-item scale to measure procrastination. He also has a second example of a multiple-item scale to measure attitudes towards mathematics. As a general rule, the descriptive status survey is more likely to be concerned with responses to individual items. The relationships-between-variables-survey is more likely to be concerned with multiple-item scaling.

The role of pilot testing

Unless your survey questionnaire, in its entirety, is the same as one already used and field tested, there is pilot testing to be done. The form and extent of the pilot testing that is required varies from situation to situation and is mainly a function of how much of the instrument is new. However, there are three general objectives to guide the pilot testing:

- Newly written items and questions need to be tested for comprehension, clarity, ambiguity and difficulty in responding to. We need to ensure that our data collection questions 'work', in the sense that people can quickly, easily and confidently respond to them.
- The whole questionnaire needs to be tested for length, and for time and difficulty to complete.
- The proposed data collection process itself, of which the questionnaire is the main feature, needs testing. This includes issues of access and approach, ethical issues, covering letters, and so on. Care taken during this stage is likely to help increase response rates.

Preliminary work for developing the questionnaire may involve the use of qualitative techniques – such as open-ended interviews and focus-group interviews – as a basis for developing data collection questions. This is especially appropriate for some survey topics and enables the researcher to combine the strengths of qualitative and quantitative approaches.

The constraints you have to work within

There are a number of constraints to consider, and decisions to be made, in developing the survey questionnaire:

- It should follow on from, and fit in with, the research questions. As noted, the starting point for questionnaire development is the research questions. They provide both the conceptual map for the questionnaire and the list of information which will be required.

- Should it be a new questionnaire, specifically developed for this project? This is a decision which needs to be made early in the research planning since it affects a lot of what follows. Guidelines for the decision are given above.

- How long should the survey questionnaire be? This is a practical issue which will strongly influence response rates and the quality of the survey data. Survey research depends on the cooperation of people in responding to the questionnaire. A major determinant of that cooperation is the length of the questionnaire. It is better to have a shorter questionnaire with higher response rates and more valid responses than a longer questionnaire where response rates and validity are jeopardised. How long is too long? This is a matter of judgement, but a questionnaire taking longer than 20–30 minutes to complete is certainly a problem. Only pilot testing can tell you how long it will take to answer your questionnaire.

- How will the questionnaire be administered? Another important decision concerns the mode of administration of the questionnaire. The options are well known and fairly limited. The main ones are through the mail, face to face, over the telephone or by way of the internet. Each has advantages and disadvantages, and the matter is discussed in section 4.2 (pp. 62–3). The point here is that this issue needs to be considered in the early stages of research planning.

- Format of questions. This is a topic with a great deal of literature and one which can be unnerving to the novice researcher. It is such a big topic because there are so many different ways to ask questions. Box 4.2 (p. 53) suggests some useful frameworks to guide you though this maze. Remember too that locating and using an already existing instrument solves the question-asking format problem for you.

- Ethical considerations. As always when social science researchers are collecting data from and about people, there are ethical issues to consider. They include confidentiality and anonymity, respecting people's privacy, and their right to know what will happen to the information they provide. These interact with the important issue of access to respondents and how the respondents are approached.

3.4 THE SAMPLE

The logic of surveys based on self-report questionnaires is to collect information from some group of people – or sample – in order to answer the research questions. Now we have to ask: From what group of people will data be collected, how many will they be and how will they be selected? There are logical issues involved in dealing with these sampling questions.

'Sample' itself is a technical term in research. It means a smaller subset drawn from some larger group. The technical term for that larger group is 'population'. These two technical terms – sample and population – mean quite different things from each other, and should be used carefully in research. In particular, the confused term 'sample population' should be avoided.

The usual situation in research is that we want to find out something about a population of people, but we can only study a sample of that population. Therefore questions of sample–population relationships arise, and especially the important question of how well a sample represents the population from which it was drawn. This is important because we usually wish to generalise our survey findings from the sample back to the population. This is the representativeness–generalisability issue and is discussed later in this section.[4]

The area of sampling is where the small-scale survey project may differ substantially from the surveys described in many research methods books. The literature usually describes ideal-type survey sampling strategies, implicitly assuming unlimited time, resources and access to people. The graduate student, however, is very often working alone, with limited time, resources and access to people. In this situation, the student researcher often has to settle for a small sample, manageable within the limits of the project, which is accessible. Indeed, some type of 'accidental' or 'convenience sampling' (terms usually associated with qualitative research) is often the strategy for obtaining a sample for the small-scale surveys which are the focus of this book.

Despite this, it is important to realise that there is a well-developed body of sampling theory (see, for example, Babbie, 1990; Alreck and Settle, 1995; Sapsford, 1999; and also Appendix 1). Since, for any survey, there is a theoretically ideal sample, a useful exercise is to think through, in an ideal-type way, the sample and the sampling process for the study under consideration – in other words, to consider this question: In an ideal world, with ample resources and access, what sample would I choose for this survey, and why? Of course, the answer to this question then has to be set against what is possible and feasible within the constraints of this project.

The 'why' part of the above question is important, because it forces consideration of the logic of the sample and of sample selection. Too often, in my experience, proposed projects have no logic behind their sampling.[5] I believe that the logic of the study, as expressed in its research questions, should flow through to its sampling strategy, rather than the sample being an afterthought. This is part of the internal validity of a project.

The focus in this book is on small-scale surveys which study the relationships between variables. This implies a logical principle to guide sample selection and at the same time illustrates the point made above – that the logic of a study should include its sampling. The principle is:

> *Where possible, select the sample so that any relationship between the variables has the maximum chance to be observed.*

The practical implication of this is selecting the sample to maximise the variation in the independent variable. This principle is illustrated in Box 3.3.

Box 3.3   Maximising independent variable variance

Selecting a sample so that independent variable variance is maximised gives the greatest chance for any independent–dependent variable relationships to be observed. This is adapting a principle of experimental design to the non-experimental quantitative survey situation.

Example 1

If we want to study the effect of smoking (IV) on measures of health (DV), the best comparison is between people who smoke a great deal and those who do not smoke at all. This implies non-probability, deliberate or purposive sampling rather than probability based random or representative sampling. We deliberately select people who smoke a great deal for comparison with those who do not smoke at all.

Example 2

If we want to see whether class size (IV) affects teaching strategy (DV), the best comparison is between relatively big classes (say 40 students or more) and relatively small classes (say 20 students or less). We deliberately select class sizes to strengthen the comparison.

Maximising independent variable variance means deliberate or purposive sampling rather than random sampling. A common misapprehension among beginning researchers is that all samples must be randomly chosen. However, the logic of some studies, especially those studying the relationship between variables, is that the sample should be more deliberately or purposively chosen. The point is that the strategy behind the sampling – especially whether it is purposive or random – should follow from the overall logic of the study, and of its research questions.

The concept of random sampling is closely tied to the concepts of generalisability and representativeness. A sample which is representative of its population provides generalisability of its results to that population. One which is not representative does not provide that generalisability. Random sampling is a common strategy (though not always in the form of simple random sampling) for ensuring representativeness.

Thus there are two different questions here. In the proposed survey:

- How important is variability, especially variability in the independent variable(s)?
- How important is representativeness?

These can usually be answered by reference back to the research questions. Often, in a small-scale survey, there is a tension between these two sampling questions – you can't do both. When that is the case, I recommend ensuring variability in the sample so that relationships between variables have the maximum chance to show up. Since the research questions are the point of reference for deciding what sort of sampling is required, Box 3.4 shows examples of questions which require representative samples and others where purposive sampling would be better.

These two types of question – variability and representativeness – are not necessarily independent of each other. Even when the focus is on the relationship between variables, and the sampling is appropriately purposive, the question of generalisability is still present. Thus, when a purposive sample demonstrates a relationship, it is still necessary to ask how generalisable that relationship is to some wider population, or across other samples. But there are limits to what any one survey can do, especially a small-scale project. One such survey may well demonstrate a relationship between variables. It cannot itself show how widespread that relationship is. That becomes a question for further research and for further survey projects.

It is useful to consider the ideal sample for any survey. In practice, however, student researchers may have to take whatever sample they

---

Box 3.4 Research questions and sampling

Some types of research question require purposive sampling where independent variable variance is maximised. These are relationship questions.

Examples:

- What is the relationship between hours of study (IV) and grade-point average (DV)?
  - maximise sample variance in hours of study
- What is the relationship between rate of promotion (IV) and job satisfaction (DV)?
  - maximise sample variance in rate of promotion

In both of these cases, purposive sampling is appropriate.

Other types of research questions require a representative sample, since they are directed at generalisability. These are distribution questions.

Examples:

- How widespread is the view that this organisation needs a change of direction?
- To what extent do union members think they have had sufficient opportunity to participate in policy formation?

In both of these cases, representative samples are required.

---

can get – in other words, the sample may have to be 'selected' on a 'convenience' basis. Sometimes the worth of a project is dismissed because such a convenience sample was used or is proposed. However, I believe that we can learn something useful from almost any sample as long as the research is carefully and thoroughly carried out. Of course we need to know about any biases in a sample, about any way in which this sample may be atypical, and we need to be very careful about making exaggerated claims for generalisability from such samples. But any well-conducted survey can contribute something and, as noted in Chapter 2 (p. 22), research usually builds knowledge cumulatively, across many studies.

Thus, the two general questions about the sampling in a survey are:

- What is the sampling strategy and how does it fit with the logic of the project?
- How important are the issues of variability in the independent variables and representativeness?

Two more specific questions about the sampling then follow:

- How big should the sample be and why?
- How should the sample be selected and why?

One other point needs to be noted here. It concerns the important relationship between the number of variables and the sample size. Intuitively, it makes sense that the more variables we are studying, the greater the sample size needs to be. Technically, this comes down to the number of cases in different cells, when cross classifications are made on the independent variables. The more independent variables there are, the more cells there will be in the cross classifications and the larger the sample size needs to be to ensure a reasonable number in each cell. For practical purposes, this means that small-scale surveys have to be careful in the number of variables they include.

3.5 DATA COLLECTION STRATEGY

In the type of survey we are considering – small-scale, quantitative and focused on relationships between variables – the self-report questionnaire is the data collection instrument to be administered to the sample selected. The question of the data collection strategy is about the actual process to be used: How will the questionnaire be administered?

Many surveys use the self-administered questionnaire method, where the questionnaire is administered to respondents – often by mail, but sometimes by other methods[6] – together with appropriate covering letters and instructions for completing and returning the questionnaire. 'Self-administered' here means that the researcher does not actually meet respondents face to face. Variations of this method include face-to-face administration (one-to-one or one-to-group, as in a meeting), administration of the questionnaire by telephone and, more recently, electronically by email or internet.[7]

The data collection strategy – the way the data are collected – can strongly influence the quality of the data. Quality of the data in turn is a major determinant of the credibility of research findings and is discussed in the next section. Various writers analyse the strengths and weaknesses of the different strategies (for example, Babbie, 1990; Alreck and Settle, 1995; Czaja and Blair, 1996; Edwards et al., 1997). In each survey project, the alternative means of questionnaire distribution have to be assessed in the light of circumstances and practical constraints so that it is not easy to say in general which alternative is best. But with reference to the quality of the data, four general points can be made:

- better planning for data collection, including a professional and ethical access and approach to respondents, leads to better quality of data;
- greater effort in data collection means better quality of data;
- more researcher control in data collection means better quality of data;
- if the choice arises when considering data collection strategies, it is better to have a smaller body of good data than a larger body of poor data.

The data collection strategy which is chosen should be realistic in the circumstances of the study, and the researcher should also identify a realistic time frame for data collection. A common problem in survey research is when to 'draw the line' which brings the data collection phase to an end. This should be considered in the research planning stage rather than as an afterthought. The decision about when to end the data collection is related to the choice of data collection strategies.

The most common method of data collection in the type of survey we consider here is the self-administered, self-report questionnaire, often distributed by mail, sometimes by other methods. The implementation of the data collection strategy in Chapter 4 therefore concentrates on this.

Quality of data

Empirical research should strive for the best possible quality of data. Since findings and conclusions from any study are only as good as the data on which they are based, quality of data should be an overriding consideration in deciding the various issues raised in this chapter.

What does quality of data mean? What distinguishes good survey data from poor survey data? We can look at quality of data first from a technical point of view, using the concepts of reliability and validity, and then from a non-technical point of view, under the headings of response rates and frame of mind of the respondent.

Reliability

Generally, reliability means stability of response.[8] Would the same respondents answer the same questions in the same way if they were asked again? If they would, our questions provide data with high reliability. We want survey questions which produce stable responses and that depends in part on whether the questions can be consistently and straightforwardly answered using the response scales and alternatives provided. It is also related to the frame of mind – or attitude – of the respondent when answering.

Validity

Generally, validity means whether the data represent what we think they represent. The general validity question for survey questionnaire data is: Do the responses which I have, and which I will score, really measure the variables which I think they measure? As well as the validity of the questions and items themselves, the issue here is whether respondents answer honestly and conscientiously. This again depends partly on the respondent's frame of mind and attitude. It also involves whether they are able to answer the questions we ask, an issue to be investigated in pilot testing.

Response rates

This means the proportion of the selected sample who complete the questionnaire. If questionnaires are distributed to 300 people and responses are received from 100 of these, the response rate is 33%. Response rates in the 30–40% range or less, are not uncommon when mail distribution is the chosen data collection strategy. This creates a problem. Earlier, we were concerned with whether a given sample might be representative of a population. A low response rate now raises the additional question of whether the responses received are representative of the sample chosen or are in some way biased. Clearly, higher response rates are better, and I believe survey researchers should strive for response rates of at least 60%. Once again, this will require planning and preparation rather than being treated as an afterthought. Methods for maximising response rates needs to be considered well before the actual data collection. References to numerous suggestions for maximising response rates are given in Box 3.5.

Box 3.5   Maximising response rates in a survey

Useful discussions on maximising survey response rates with self-administered questionnaires are found in:

- Alreck and Settle (1995: 183–209)
- Babbie (1990: 176–86)
- Braverman and Slater (1996: 24–5)
- Czaja and Blair (1996: 31–49)
- Edwards et al. (1997: 91–100)
- Fink and Kosecoff (1998: 5–6, 50)
- Moser and Kalton (1979: 262–9)
- Schofield (1986: 25–56)
- Suskie (1996: 69–90)

These discussions include a variety of suggestions for improving response rates. General principles covered include:

- Make response rates a subject for planning in the data collection, not a subject for *post hoc* remedy.
- Carefully plan access to respondents, pre-notification to them of the survey and covering letters.
- Similarly, carefully plan procedures for the return of the survey and for follow-up and reminder contact.
- Be aware that the design, appearance, lay out, length and readability of the questionnaire influence response rates.

In addition, Edwards et al. (1997: 99–100) summarise several meta-analyses investigating the effects of different factors on survey response rates and include a table of 14 specific suggestions for maximising response rates. You need to assess the relevance of such specific suggestions to your particular survey situation.

Frame of mind or attitude of respondent

When the respondent sits down to answer the questionnaire, the researcher, ideally, wants the respondent's frame of mind to be cooperative and the respondent to answer honestly and conscientiously. Maximising the chances of this happening again depends on careful planning and preparation by the researcher. It includes such issues as:

- making sure the approach to respondents is as professional and as inviting as possible;
- taking all appropriate ethical considerations into account;
- ensuring that the questionnaire is as attractively presented as possible;
- through appropriate pilot testing, ensuring that the data collection questions work.

These are common-sense but important issues. The more positive and cooperative the respondent when answering the questionnaire, the higher the reliability, validity and response rate. The researcher needs to do all that is possible to ensure a positive and cooperative frame of mind.

Quality of data needs to be set against quantity of data, an issue to be considered in the size of the questionnaire and the size of the sample. A greater quantity of data is not, in itself, necessarily good. Indeed, quantitative survey research has seen a swing from large sample 'number crunching' in the 1960s to smaller, more targeted samples in later years. The issue is not more data, it is better data – hence the idea that it is better to have a smaller body of good quality data than a larger body of data of doubtful quality. This does not contradict the desirability of high response rates. Having taken overall quantity of data into account in the sample selection stage, it is clearly desirable to achieve as high a response rate as possible.

3.6 DATA ANALYSIS STRATEGY

Once the data have been collected, how will they be analysed? As usual, we are taken back immediately to the central role of the research questions. The research questions tell the researcher what data are needed. They also indicate or imply what should be done with the data to answer the questions. This means that the researcher, even when not expert in statistics, should be able to see, on a logical (rather than methodological) basis, what should be done with the data in order to answer the questions. I believe this point is important, and often overlooked. Of course methodological expertise is important in this work. But too often, especially for the research student who is not expert in statistics, this can obscure the logical strategy which must underlie the statistical analysis. I believe, therefore, that in the proposal which precedes the survey the researcher should be able to describe on a logical basis how the analysis of the data would proceed in order to answer the research questions.[9]

Before undertaking the analysis itself, the survey data need preparation – data cleaning and data entry. Data cleaning refers to the tidying up of the data set before the analysis itself begins. Questionnaire responses need to be proofread by the researcher, and decisions made about unclear responses, situations where a respondent may have answered more than one alternative, and missing data. Once that is done, the questionnaire responses need to be entered into the computer for electronic data processing. Questions of design, layout and format will have to be answered in preparing data for processing. Those questions have become easier to deal with, because of the widespread availability of processing packages, their clear instructions as to how to format data, and their ability to work with data sets entered in various formats. Also, increasing use is made today of scannable questionnaires, whereby responses can be automatically read into the computer.

For the type of quantitative survey in focus here, there are three main data analysis steps which can usually be applied and which follow a logical order. They are:

- summarising and reducing data – creating the variables;
- descriptive level analysis – the distribution of the variables across the sample;
- relationships analysis – relationships between the variables – first bivariately, then (as appropriate) jointly.

The last two steps follow the earlier distinction (Chapter 2, p. 17) between questions of distribution and questions of relationship, and all three steps are presented in more detail in Chapter 4 (pp. 63–5). As Chapter 4 points out, the analysis of survey data, especially when the data set is complex, is a process of successively summarising and distilling the data in order to reach substantive conclusions, all within the framework of providing answers to the research questions. The systematic use of tables facilitates the organisation, interpretation and communication of the survey results.

3.7 REVIEW CONCEPTS

hierarchy of concepts – levels of abstraction
survey objectives
general research questions
specific research questions
data collection questions

the empirical criterion for research questions
conceptual framework

definitions of variables
conceptual definitions
operational definitions
major variables – multiple-item scales
pilot testing
sample versus population
sampling strategy
deliberate or purposive sampling – maximising independent variable
variance
random sampling – representativeness, generalisability
sample size

data collection
self-administered, self-report questionnaire
quality of data (reliability, validity, response rates)

data analysis
data cleaning
data entry
summarising data
descriptive analysis – distribution of the variables
relationships between the variables

NOTES

1. Grounded theory analysis is a prominent example of this point from qualitative research. It is based on raising the conceptual level of specific pieces of qualitative empirical data (see Punch, 1998: 210–18).
2. I use the term 'survey' to refer to the whole project we are describing, with the seven main elements shown in Chapter 2. By 'questionnaire', I mean the data collection instrument used in the survey. The 'survey questionnaire' thus means the questionnaire used in the survey.
3. See for example:

    Bearden, W.O. (1999) *Handbook of Marketing Scales*. Chicago: American Marketing Association.
    Bonjean, C.M., Hill, R.J. and McLemore, S.D. (1967) *Sociological Measurement*. San Francisco: Chandler.
    Bowling, A. (1991) *Measuring Health: A Review of Quality of Life Measurement Scales*. Philadelphia: Open University Press.

Bruner, G.C. and Hansel, P.J. (1992) *Marketing Scales Handbook: A Compilation of Multi-Item Measures.* Chicago: American Marketing Association.

Conoley, J.C. and Impara, J.C. (eds) (1995) *Twelfth Mental Measurements Yearbook.* Lincoln, NB: Buros Institute of Mental Measurements, University of Nebraska Press.

Frank-Stromborg, M. (ed.) (1988) *Instruments for Clinical Nursing Research.* Norwalk, CT: Appleton & Lange.

Goldman, B.A. and Mitchell, D.F. (eds) (1996) *Directory of Unpublished Experimental Mental Measures,* Vol. 6. Washington, DC: American Psychological Association.

Hersen, M. and Bellack, A.S. (eds) (1988) *Measures for Clinical Practice.* New York: The Free Press.

Maddox, T. (ed.) (1997) *Tests: A Comprehensive Reference for Assessments in Psychology, Education and Business,* 4th edition. Austin, TX: Pro Ed.

McDowell, I. and Newell, C. (1987) *Measuring Health: A Guide to Rating Scales and Questionnaires.* Oxford: Oxford University Press.

Miller, D.C. (1991) *Handbook of Research Design and Social Measurement,* 5th edn. Newbury Park, CA: Sage.

Murphy, L.E., Close, C.J. and Impara, J.C. (1994) *Tests in Print IV: An Index to Tests, Test Reviews, and the Literature on Specific Tests,* Vol. 1. Lincoln, NB: Buros Institute of Mental Measurements, University of Nebraska Press.

Price, J.M. and Mueller, C.W. (1986) *Handbook of Organizational Measures.* Marshfield, MA: Pitman.

Shaw, M.E. and Wright, J.W. (1967) *Scales for the Measurement of Attitudes.* Ann Arbor, MI: Institute of Social Research.

Stewart, A.L. and Ware, J.E. (eds) (1992) *Measuring Functioning and Well-Being.* Durham, NC: Duke University Press.

Straus, M.A. and Brown, B.W. (1978) *Family Measurement Techniques: Abstracts of Published Instruments, 1935–1974,* revised edn. Minneapolis: University of Minnesota Press.

Streiner, D.R. and Norman, G. (1995) *Health Measurement Scales: A Practical Guide to their Development and Use.* Oxford: Oxford University Press.

Sweetland, R.C. and Keyser, D.J. (1986) *Tests: A Comprehensive Reference for Assessments in Psychology, Education, and Business,* 2nd edn. Kansas City, MO: Test Corporation of America.

4. It is possible for the survey, even a small-scale survey, to collect its data from a total population of people. Examples would be all employees of a particular company or all teachers in a particular school. If there is no attempt to generalise beyond that group of people, it is appropriate to label the group a population. Whenever we seek to generalise beyond the data we have collected, the group is a sample drawn from a population. Studying samples is much more common in quantitative surveys than studying populations.

5. In both quantitative and qualitative research.

6. For example, questionnaires may be distributed in the workplace or at a meeting or, as in a school, to parents by way of children, and so on.

7. Administering the survey questionnaire electronically, while potentially an appealing prospect, is, however, not straightforward. Special problems can arise as described, for example, by Dillman (1999).

8. I am concentrating here on the stability aspect of reliability. With multiple-item scales, reliability also has an internal consistency aspect (see pp. 32–4 and pp. 60–1).

9. This point about methodological expertise at the proposal stage is discussed in *Developing Effective Research Proposals* (Punch, 2000: 60–2).

4

Elements of the Survey: Implementation

CONTENTS

Chapter 3 described the main elements of the survey. This chapter now gives a set of steps for putting each element into practice, using different parts of the examples in Chapter 6 for illustration. These steps are interrelated and interdependent, and they need to be congruent with each other. This is part of the internal validity of the project, by which the survey is developed as a coherent whole. As the steps are presented, some recurrent issues typically faced by beginning researchers are described, and guidelines for dealing with them are given.

4.1 DEVELOPING OBJECTIVES AND RESEARCH QUESTIONS

The hierarchy of concepts presented in detail in Chapter 3, and repeated below, is a useful tool at this stage.

- research area;
- research topic;

- survey objectives;
- general research questions;
- specific research questions;
- data collection questions.

In line with this, once the research area and topic are identified, the steps to go through are:

1 Develop a clear statement of the objective(s) of the survey.
2 Develop the general research questions from the objectives.
3 Develop the specific research questions from the general research questions.
4 Ensure each specific research question meets the empirical criterion.
5 Show the conceptual framework for the survey.
6 Develop data collection questions from the specific research questions.

Steps 1, 2 and 3 above are interrelated and may well be done simultaneously rather than sequentially. Also, the researcher may work downwards from objectives to research questions, upwards from research questions to objectives, or – more likely – both ways interactively. 'Working downwards' – or deductively – means beginning with a general statement of the objectives and then making that statement more specific, moving down to general and then specific research questions. 'Working upwards' – or inductively – means beginning with specific questions of interest and then moving up to more general statements of questions and then objectives.

As the specific research questions of step 3 are being developed, the empirical criterion should be applied, making modifications to the phrasing of the research questions, as needed to bring them into line with this criterion. With the empirical criterion satisfied for each specific research question, the focus can move to the data collection questions, and the important connections between questions, variables and data can be developed. Box 3.1 (p. 28) shows the simple example of Chapter 6 developed in this way.

In the actual planning of the research, students sometimes have difficulty with the distinction between general and specific research questions. While I recommend the distinction as a very useful practical and pedagogical device, I realise that it does not always work as clearly as is suggested here. If it is too difficult, this particular distinction can be de-emphasised – it often re-emerges more clearly later on. But even if this is done, it is worth keeping in mind the general framework provided by this hierarchy.

Once the specific research questions are finalised, the conceptual framework for the survey can be described. In the process of working through the steps shown above, the conceptual framework and general and specific research questions are likely to be developed side by side, each influencing the other. The conceptual framework for both examples in Chapter 6 is shown in Box 4.1 (p. 52).

Step 6 above, developing data collection questions, takes us into questionnaire development.

4.2 DEVELOPING THE QUESTIONNAIRE

This step of developing the questionnaire operationalises the research questions. In terms of the hierarchy of concepts, it is where the data collection questions are formulated. The conceptual framework provides the conceptual map behind the questionnaire. If each research question clearly meets the empirical criterion, this important step of developing the questionnaire – while complicated in that it involves a number of sub-steps and technical considerations – is also straightforward. It is even more straightforward if you are able to use already existing instruments, in whole or in part, as discussed in Chapter 3.

The nine general steps in developing the questionnaire are:

1 Go through each specific research question and decide what information is necessary to answer it; use this to make a list of the variables involved.
2 Provide conceptual definitions for the variables, as appropriate.
3 For each variable, decide whether the information required is factual, cognitive, affective or behavioural. Box 4.2 gives examples of frameworks for organising the types of information typically collected in surveys.
4 Decide whether each variable is categorical or continuous, in the way that it is to be measured. This is an important distinction, and one of the technical issues discussed below. It was also described in Chapter 2 (pp. 19–20).
5 For each variable, decide whether the data will be in the form of a single indicator, or of multiple items making up a scale. This enables you to decide how many data collection questions are planned for each variable. The special case of multiple items to make up a scale is discussed as a technical issue below.
6 Draw up a table summarising the last three points above. Cross check this table against your constraints, especially those relating to

Box 4.1   Conceptual frameworks

Simple example (Chapter 6)

Objective: to investigate the relationship between mental ability and time on task as independent variables and achievement as dependent variable.

General and specific research questions: see Chapter 6, p. 81.

List of variables: mental ability (MA), time on task (TT), achievement.

Conceptual framework:

Independent variables	Dependent variable

MA
TT } ⟶ Achievement

Complex example (Chapter 6)

Objective: to investigate the relationship between mental ability and time on task as independent variables and achievement as dependent variable, after controlling for alienation, in the context of differing social class levels.

General and specific research questions: see Chapter 6, p. 91.

List of variables: mental ability (MA), time on task (TT), achievement, social class (SES), alienation.

Conceptual framework:

Context variable	Independent variables	Control variable	Dependent variable

SES   { MA
         TT } ⟶ [Alienation] ⟶ Achievement

Box 4.2 Frameworks for organising survey information

[i]   Cognitive   Affective   Behavioural
      variables   variables   variables

[ii] Knowledge   Attitudes   Practices

Frameworks [i] and [ii] are similar, using different terms for the same ideas. Both can be put together, with the earlier idea of social properties, as in [iii] below.

[iii] Social property   Cognitive   Affective   Behavioural
      variables   variables   variables   variables

      (or   (or   (or   (or
      demographics)   knowledge)   attitudes)   practices)

[iv] An alternative framework based on concepts commonly used in quantitative surveys is provided by Alreck and Settle (1995: 11–24).

      Attitudes   Needs   Affiliations
      Images   Behaviour   Demographic
      Decisions   Lifestyles

---

size of questionnaire and time required to complete it. Remember that these are a major determinant of response rates. Often trimming is needed at this point.

7 Formulate the items, to give a draft form of the questionnaire. For those parts of the questionnaire which use items from other instruments, this step is straightforward. For those items and questions being developed specifically for this survey, we need to keep in mind that there are many different ways to phrase items or ask questions, and that this issue has been written about extensively by measurement theorists. Some useful references which contain commonly accepted guidelines are shown in Box 4.3. The general principle shown as point (8) below (p. 61) summarises these guidelines.

8 Pilot test the draft form of the questionnaire. Two forms of pilot testing of new questions and items are desirable. First, with a small group of respondents where the emphasis is on improving clarity, removing ambiguity, confirming interpretations and checking that

---

Box 4.3 Guidelines for question asking and item writing

Useful references on this topic are:

Babbie (1990: 127–46)	Lewins (1992)
Converse and Presser (1986)	Oppenheim (1992)
Czaja and Blair (1996: 51–73)	Sapsford (1999: 103–8)
Edwards et al. (1997: 24–38)	Sudman and Bradburn (1982)
Fink (1995)	Suskie (1996: 24–43)
	Tuckman (1999: 236–58)

In addition to the specific guidelines summarised in point 8 (p. 53), four general points apply:

- Use other instruments and items from other instruments, where appropriate.
- Think carefully about the indicators which, all would agree, represent the variable being measured.
- Pilot test new questions, items and scales with potential respondents.
- Have your questionnaire reviewed by experts.

---

respondents can easily answer the questions. Secondly, with a larger group where the distribution of item responses and inter-item relationships can be investigated. This second step is especially important if a new multiple-item scale has been developed. As noted in Chapter 3, the pilot testing should assess the questions and items, the overall questionnaire and the process proposed for its administration.

9   Use pilot test results to finalise the questionnaire. Unsatisfactory items can now be modified, replaced or deleted, as can scale items which do not discriminate between respondents. This last point is discussed as technical issue (6) below (p. 60).

Eight technical issues

Questionnaire development for surveys investigating relationships between variables necessarily involves some technical aspects of measurement. The seven technical issues discussed in this section are ones that I have found occur repeatedly, and are especially important for beginning researchers planning and conducting quantitative surveys.

They are related to each other, but they can also occur as separate issues when students are doing this sort of work. Most of them concern quality of the survey data, with implications for the analysis, and the suggestions I make in this section aim to maximise that quality. In the discussion, I have emphasised the logical rather than the technical aspects of these issues.

1   Categorical versus continuous variables

This easy-to-understand distinction between categorical and continuous has important implications for the analysis of survey data, and the researcher needs to be clear which variables are categorical and which are continuous. Most quantitative surveys will contain both types of variable.

Categorical data require non-parametric statistical techniques for analysis, whereas continuous data can be analysed using more powerful parametric statistical techniques. The reason for this is that, while the numbers 1, 2, 3 and so on can be used to represent the different response categories in a categorical variable, they are not in this case ordered numbers with meaningful intervals between them. Instead, they are only being used as category labels. Therefore the arithmetic operations on which parametric techniques depend – such as addition (and averaging), subtraction, multiplication and division – do not apply. Most commonly in survey research at this level, this means that we use contingency tables to study the relationship between the categorical variables rather than the more widely known Pearson product–moment correlation.

To help clarify this distinction between categorical and continuous variables, the key question to ask is: When responses are being coded using numbers, are the responses scaled or not? That is, if response categories are being scored 1, 2, 3 and so on, do the different numbers represent differing degrees or levels or quantities of the variable? If they do, the variable is being scaled, and continuous variable correlation can be used in the analysis.[1] If they do not, the variable is not being scaled, and contingency tables (or some other non-parametric method)[2] should be used in the analysis. For example, gender may be scored 1 for female and 2 for male (or vice versa). But these numbers do not represent quantities, the variable is not being scaled. Again, country of birth may be scored 1 for Australia, 2 for India, 3 for China, and so on. Again, the numbers do not represent quantities and the variable is not being scaled. The numbers are used only as labels to identify categories.

On the other hand, consider a frequency-of-behaviour question such as this one from a survey of voter behaviour (Alreck and Settle, 1995: 363).

Question: How often do you do each of the following things?

Response: (Scoring)	Always (5)	Often (4)	Sometimes (3)	Rarely (2)	Never (1)
Seek information about candidates					
Vote in local elections					
Vote along strict party lines					
Contribute money to candidates					
Volunteer to work on campaigns					

Assume it is scored as shown, with 5 for always, 4 for often, and so on. These numbers do now represent quantities and the variable is being scaled – as the numbers increase, so does the (reported) frequency of occurrence of the behaviour described in the item. This is therefore a continuous variable.

There is nothing wrong with the numerical scoring of categorical variables, using numbers merely as category labels. It is done all the time. But parametric or continuous variable techniques – such as means and standard deviations for distribution analysis and product moment correlation for relationships analysis – should not be used in analysing such variables.[3] Other techniques are required.

2 Dichotomous response versus scaled response

This issue is closely related to the previous one. Some questions require a dichotomous response system. Examples, adapted from the Maryland Crime Survey (Czaja and Blair, 1996), are:

- Are you
  1. Male   2. Female
- Within the past year have you had a burglar alarm installed in your home?
  1. Yes   2. No
- Within the past year have you purchased a gun or other weapon for protection?
  1. Yes   2. No

Most of the time, these are knowledge or factual questions.

Other questions can be used with either a dichotomous response or a scaled response system – the developer of the questionnaire has a choice. An example is:

- Do you like doing research?
  1. Yes   2. No
  versus
- To what extent do you like doing research?
  1. A great deal   2. Quite a lot   3. Only a little   4. Not at all

Often, these are affective or behavioural questions.

When faced with this choice in questionnaire construction, a good general rule is to use scaled responses – rating scales – where possible. The reasons are that scaled responses produce more information and more variance, that they are easier to analyse and that the analysis can go further. The qualification is that the additional variance produced needs to be meaningful and reliable variance. That is, response scale categories need to be realistic and respondents need to be able to choose their response from among the alternatives in a stable and straightforward way. Such rating scales have flexibility and wide applicability, and are an effective way to get survey information. Different types of rating scale response category are shown in Box 4.4 below, and rating scales are discussed in points (4) and (5).

3 Respondents supply versus respondents rate

Another related problem arises in this type of quantitative survey when respondents are asked to supply content or information rather than simply to respond to rating scales with the content or information already supplied. Two examples are:

- A researcher wants to survey the reasons parents have for choosing a particular school for their child. The survey questionnaire asks parents to supply the three most important reasons in their choice.
- A researcher wants to find the most-liked and least-liked features of a training programme undertaken by staff in a hospital. The questionnaire asks respondents to nominate the three most-liked features and the three least-liked features of the programme.

While useful information can be collected using this more open-ended way of asking questions, the problem is that it is difficult to deal with information in this format at anything more than a simple descriptive level. It is difficult, in other words, to apply more powerful analytical techniques, and therefore difficult to relate this information to other variables. Yet that is the main purpose of the type of quantitative survey we are considering here.

In both cases, therefore, an alternative worth considering in a quantitative survey is to supply the content or information – in the first case the possible reasons, in the second case the possible features – and have respondents rate them. This requires some preliminary investigation and means splitting the research into two stages. First, using qualitative techniques – for example the focus group interview, an especially useful tool in this situation (Morgan, 1988; Stewart and Shamdasani, 1990; Krueger, 1994) – get as full a picture as possible of likely reasons or features. Often, saturation is reached in this exercise quite quickly – that is, a comprehensive view of the main reasons or features can emerge quite soon. Summarise each reason or feature into a word or short phrase. Secondly, in the questionnaire ask respondents to rate each reason or feature on a scale using appropriate wording (see sections (4) and (5) below).[4]

If this is done, every respondent has responded to each reason or feature. In this way, the data set is much more complete and much better for analysis. Especially, it is much easier to study systematically relationships between the variables. Splitting the process into these two steps involves more work, but the data are better and the analysis can go further.

4   Types of scaled response

There are many ways responses to questions can be scaled. Which way is most appropriate will depend mainly on the way the question or item is worded. Box 4.4 shows some common types of survey questions and their scaled response formats. The possibilities are not limited to what is shown in the box. Indeed, one of the advantages of this type of question asking is its flexibility, and thus its applicability to a wide range of situations. For example, importance ratings are shown in the box. These can easily be adapted to cover other characteristics of interest. The survey researcher needs to select the type of question and the response scale which are most appropriate for the topic and research questions of the particular project.[5]

5   Number of points on the response scale

Given the importance of rating scales, another recurrent and often problematic issue is the number of points to have on the response scale used. Two guidelines can help with this issue.

Box 4.4   Some types of scaled responses

Points along the scale continuum (four point scale)

Type of scale	1	2	3	4
Agreement	Strongly disagree	Disagree	Agree	Strongly agree
Satisfaction	Very dissatisfied	Dissatisfied	Satisfied	Very satisfied
Effectiveness	Very ineffective	Ineffective	Effective	Very effective

Points along the scale continuum (five point scale)

Type of scale	1	2	3	4	5
Frequency	Never	Seldom	About half the time	Often	Always
Quality	Very poor	Poor	Average	Good	Very good
Importance	Not at all	A little	Reasonably	Very	Extremely

Other samples of response scales can be found in Alreck and Settle (1995: 111–42) and Czaja and Blair (1996: 70).

The first is that a greater number of scale points is likely to produce more variance, which is desirable, for the reasons given in point (6) below. But, as noted in point (2) above, that variance has to be reliable and meaningful. Reliable here means stable – respondents would answer the same way if asked the same questions again. Meaningful means the related idea that respondents can confidently (and quickly) select the one response category for each item which applies to them. Several of the examples in the Box 4.4 show a four-point scale, and this is a recommended starting point. Whether more points will work depends on the type of question and respondent, and can best be answered by a combination of common sense and pilot testing. Thus you will sometimes see six-point agreement–disagreement scales (very strongly agree, strongly agree, agree, disagree, strongly disagree, very strongly disagree), or ten-point importance rating scales.[6] Try them out in pilot testing to see how well they work in your situation.

The second guideline is to be sure that all points used fall on the response scale. Whatever categories are used, the rule is that all points should clearly lie on the response scale, not that there should be any particular number of points. As shown in Box 4.4, the number of scale points could be four, five or more.[7]

6 Producing variability

When we are investigating the relationships between variables we are basically asking whether the variables vary together, or co-vary – whether they share common variance. Therefore it is important that our measurements produce variance in the variables. If our measure of a variable produces no variance, by definition that variable cannot co-vary with another variable. In this case we would conclude – erroneously – that the variables are not related. The correct conclusion really is that we don't know whether or not they are related since our measure was not sensitive enough to produce variability between people.[8]

Our measurements are made up of questions and items, so it is the questions and items themselves which need to produce variance. Questions and items produce variance by differentiating between people. In other words, we need to make sure that people do not all (or nearly all) answer the same way to a particular question or item. Obviously, this is best checked by pilot testing new questions and items. One important criterion we can use in assessing a new item is therefore the extent to which it produces variability.[9]

7 Subscales with multiple items

When multiple items are being used to create a variable, special considerations are involved. Essentially, these arise because an overall or aggregate score for the variable is to be obtained by adding responses to the individual items which make up the measure of the variable.[10] This means that we have to be sure we are adding 'like with like'. We have to be sure that each item really is an indicator of the variable we wish to measure. In technical terms, we need to show that the items which make up the variable are consistent with each other, and therefore that the scale itself is internally consistent. We take care to try to ensure this in scale construction, using content validity (Black, 1999: 231–2) to check that each item represents an indicator of the variable. In the analysis of responses, we need to demonstrate empirically the internal consistency of a multiple-item scale. A suitable technique for doing that is based on the correlations of the scale items with each other, and the correlation between each item and the total score. The degree of inter-item correlation is also summarised by coefficient alpha, probably the widely used measure of the internal consistency of a scale (Black, 1999: 279). Suggestions for further reading about the technical issues involved in multiple-item scaling and about internal consistency reliability are given in Appendix 1.

8 A general principle

Earlier, in Box 4.3, several references were given to guidelines for question and item writing. At a general level, this section now summarises those guidelines. For quantitative questionnaires, and especially when measuring variables, the general principle is that we need questions and items to which people find it easy and straightforward to respond, which don't require them to analyse and ponder at great length, and which don't get into an 'it depends' style of thinking. Ways we can try to achieve that include:

- keeping questions and items short and as simply worded as possible;
- ensuring that each item and question carries only one idea;
- avoiding negatives and double negatives;
- using language that is clear, unambiguous, relevant and appropriate, and unbiased.

Two points follow from this principle. First, it clearly restricts the sorts of things we can measure in a quantitative survey questionnaire. We cannot, for example, measure complex issues, each having many inter-related aspects, where a respondent cannot straightforwardly give a response. Nor can we realistically study, say, social processes, or examine in depth people's reactions, using quantitative survey techniques.[11] But, secondly, if we respect those restrictions, careful questionnaire development work can produce very effective measurements of our variables. We can produce excellent data to enable us to study the relationships between variables of interest. The strength of the quantitative survey is its ability to produce standardised measures to enable the systematic comparisons which are implicit in investigating the distributions of the variables and the relationships among them. This is especially the case using internally consistent multiple-item rating scales, which are effective and flexible and have wide applicability, particularly for the large class of affective variables mentioned earlier. Developing these requires the combination of careful definitional work to specify the indicators of the variable and systematic empirical cross checks using the basic principles of measurement, especially reliable variance and internal consistency. With this combination we can very effectively differentiate between people, in a reliable way, on a wide range of important variables. That is our objective in quantitative survey questionnaire measurement.

4.3   SELECTING THE SAMPLE

As noted in Chapter 3, whatever the practical constraints on a particular survey, a good strategy at the planning stage is first to determine, in ideal-type terms, what sample the project, with its overall rationale and research questions, demands and then to put that alongside the practical constraints. The following four general steps for sample selection fit in with our focus in this book on quantitative-surveys-relating-variables.

1   In ideal-type terms, decide what sample is wanted. Focus on the logic behind this decision and keep this question in mind: *Why* would this be the ideal sample for this study?
2   Decide, in particular, what the balance should be between general-isability (demanding a representative sample) and maximising independent variable variance (demanding a deliberately chosen sample). For surveys which focus on the relationships between key variables, aim to ensure variability in the independent variable(s).
3   Decide on the specific parameters of the sample. In particular:
    –   How big will the sample be?
    –   How will the sample be selected?
4   Decide on the strategy for approaching and gaining access to the people selected in the sample. Remember that this step has important consequences for the response rate and for the overall quality of the data. Remember too that many people today, as participants, suffer from research fatigue, and especially questionnaire fatigue. This makes the approach even more important. Be as professional and as inviting as possible.

Suggestions for further reading about the technical issues involved in sampling are given in Appendix 1.

4.4   COLLECTING THE DATA

Decisions about the sample and its method of selection, and about access and approach to people, interact with decisions about the actual collection of the data. As noted earlier (Chapter 3, p. 41), the important principles here are to keep control of the data collection process as much as possible and to maximise the quality of the data collected, while keeping response rates as high as possible.

The general steps here are:

1   Choose the method of administering the questionnaire. Notice that this not only involves the distribution of the questionnaire, but also its collection after completion.
2   Develop a detailed plan for the distribution and collection of the questionnaire.
3   Decide on how access to the sample will be negotiated and respondents will be approached.
4   Assuming a self-administered, self-report questionnaire, produce a covering letter, which deals with:
    • what the project is about;
    • who is conducting it and why;
    • what use will be made of the information collected;
    • how respondents have been selected;
    • confidentiality and anonymity;
    • instructions for completing and returning the questionnaire.
5   Decide on distribution methods and dates, collection methods and dates, follow-up procedures and cut-off date for the end of the data collection.
6   Pay particular attention to the question of response rates, especially if the data are to be collected by a self-administered questionnaire. The decisions in steps 1–5 above need to be taken with response rates in mind. In addition, the ideas in the references shown in Box 3.5 (p. 43) should be considered for their applicability.

4.5   ANALYSING THE DATA

This is often the part of the survey which the beginning researcher finds most daunting, especially if the survey includes a considerable number of variables. It can be made less formidable by applying the simple and logical three-part framework given in Chapter 3 (section 3.6, pp. 44–5) for analysing quantitative survey data. The three parts are:

• summarise and reduce the data – create the variables;
• show the distribution of the variables across the sample;
• analyse relationships between the variables, first bivariately, then jointly.

As shown in Chapter 6, the use of tables helps to organise the analysis and gives structure to the presentation of results. The overall focus is of course on answering the survey's research questions and some preliminary work is inevitably involved.

Thus the general steps in the analysis of quantitative survey data are:

1 Proofread completed questionnaires, deciding what to do about missing data and ambiguous or unclear responses.
2 Enter the proofread data into the computer for analysis.
3 Carry out any psychometric analysis required.[12] This will be most necessary where multiple-item scales are used to create a variable and will involve checks for internal consistency of the items. If necessary, misfitting or poorly performing items can be discarded at this point and not included in the subsequent analysis. The objective here is to make sure we have the best possible measure of each variable for use in subsequent analysis.
4 Item responses can now be aggregated into variables in accordance with the conceptual map behind the questionnaire. *This step begins with each person having a score on each question or item in the questionnaire. It is complete when each person has a score on each variable in the survey.* This is what reducing and summarising data means. For example, if a ten-item scale has been used to measure a variable, the original data set has ten scores for each person. After this step is completed, the reduced data set has one score for each person. Thus the desired situation after this step is that each person has a score on each variable in the survey. It is these variable scores which are then used in the subsequent analysis.
5 Do a descriptive analysis of all the main variables. This focuses on the distribution statements referred to in Chapter 2, and can use, as appropriate, means, standard deviations and frequency distributions. This should be done both across the whole sample and for important sub-groups within the sample, using tables to present results.
6 Investigate the bivariate relationships between the variables. Remember that the appropriate technique to use here will depend on whether the variables are continuous or categorical and, if categorical, how many categories. In general:
   - if both variables are continuous, use product–moment correlation
   - if one variable is continuous and the other categorical and dichotomous, use either point biserial correlation or t tests for the differences between group means
   - if one variable is continuous and the other categorical with more than two categories, use one-way analysis of variance for the differences between groups
   - if both variables are categorical, use contingency tables.[13]

7   Investigate joint relationships between the variables, as appropriate and as directed by the research questions. The technique to use here will depend on the way the research question is phrased, but multiple linear regression is the most likely general approach. This is described in Chapter 7 (section 7.4, pp. 106–9).

Two overall points to keep in mind about the data analysis are:

- The analysis of quantitative survey data, especially if it is a complex data set, is a process of progressively summarising and 'distilling' the data to arrive in the end at substantive conclusions about the way variables are related to each other. At the start of the analysis there is a response (scored as a number) for each respondent to every *item* and *question* on the questionnaire. The data set is thus very complex. After step 4 above, each respondent has one score for each *variable* in the survey and the data set is much simpler. Now the analysis can move on to study the distribution of variables, and then their interrelationships.
- This progressive summarising and distilling of data needs to be done in the framework of the research questions. I have stressed that they are the backbone of the survey, giving the project its coherence and organisation. They are also the best organising framework for conducting and reporting the data analysis.

Suggestions for further reading about some of the technical issues involved in data analysis are given in Appendix 1.

4.6   REVIEW CONCEPTS

internal validity of the survey
frameworks for classifying survey information
guidelines for question asking and item writing
categorical and continuous variables
dichotomous response versus scaled response
variability
multiple-item scales
internal consistency reliability
psychometric analysis

NOTES

1. I do not include ordinal level data here, where numbers are used and ordered to represent rankings. I focus in this point only on the distinction between categorising and interval level scaling because this is where I often find confusion once the data are in numerical form. If ordinal data are involved, rank order statistical techniques are required for studying the relationships between variables.
2. The method selected depends partly on the number of categories in the categorical variable – see Siegel (1956) and Black (1999).
3. The most common example of this error is the use of product moment correlation with categorical data – the correlation coefficients calculated are meaningless, except for the special case where one variable is categorical and dichotomous and the other is continuous. Here, product moment correlation reduces to point-biserial correlation (Siegel, 1956; Black, 1999).
4. The feasibility of this two-stage process for collecting data depends on how quickly saturation is reached in the qualitative stage – that is, how quickly a comprehensive view of the main reasons or features emerges. If it does not emerge quickly, with a manageable number of items, the researcher is forced to revert to the open-ended way of asking the questions where respondents supply – rather than rate – the reasons or features.
5. Another useful type of scaling derives from the semantic differential, a method of rating which is easily adaptable to many research situations. See, for example, Alreck and Settle (1995: 128–32) and Tuckman (1999: 219–22).
6. Usually, these are presented graphically, with words anchoring only the extremes. Thus

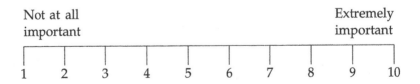

7. Sometimes 'don't know' or 'not applicable' or 'undecided' is an appropriate response. When that is the case, the important thing is to make sure it is not scored as though it were on the scale.
8. I have described the limiting case here, of no variance, to make the point. The more general point is that little variance in a measure will underestimate the relationship between variables. One of the factors

affecting the size of the coefficient of correlation between continuous variables is the amount of variance in measures of the variables.

9. We can *inspect* the amount of variability by tabulating frequency distributions of responses to a question or item. We can *measure* that variability by calculating the standard deviation of the responses, for scaled items.

10. This is the rationale of Likert or summated rating scales, the most widely used scaling procedure in social research today.

11. On a more detailed level, we must be aware that the survey information collected may be influenced by the way our questions or items are phrased. The phrasing of any question or item makes certain assumptions – or assumes a frame of reference – and this is particularly true with the structured, closed questions and items used for measurement. The researcher needs to check the validity of those assumptions with the people from whom the survey information will be collected. This highlights the importance of the way questions are asked, as is noted in Chapter 4. It also reinforces the value of using already existing instruments.

12. The technical term 'psychometric' refers to the measurement characteristics of an instrument or scale. The two psychometric characteristics I have emphasised here are the discriminatory power of items – their ability to differentiate between people – and the internal consistency of multiple-item scales.

13. If both are categorical and dichotomous, the analysis can also use the phi coefficient (Siegel, 1956; Black, 1999).

5

The Survey Report

CONTENTS

5.1 INTRODUCTION

When writing the survey report, it is important to keep in mind that its main purpose is the clear and accessible communication of the project's *objectives*, its *methods* and its *findings*.[1] Thus the essence of the report deals with these three main things, all of which follow from what has been said in earlier chapters. In certain contexts – for example, if the project is being written up as a dissertation – other sections are required. But these three sections – objectives, methods, findings – remain central in any context. For the reader of a survey report, the most important things to know are what the project was trying to find out, how it went about it, and what it found. In what follows, therefore, these sections are described first and in more detail, as the centrepiece of the report, and then other sections are put around them. The full checklist of section headings at the end of this chapter is directed particularly at the dissertation student. In the sections on objectives, methods and findings there are numerous references to the examples in Chapter 6.

One advantage of organising the survey as has been described in the earlier chapters of this book is that writing up the report and communicating about the project become fairly straightforward. Thus what you say about the objectives, methods and findings of the survey can draw closely on the way these topics have been described and set up earlier. In that sense, much of the writing for the sections of the report which deal with the objectives and methods is not new, but brings together what has been done earlier. The content of the findings section is of course new, but the framework for writing that section has already been developed through the research questions.

The benefits of an earlier detailed proposal, and of keeping full notes as the survey proceeds, become clear at this point. The organisation of the report and much of the writing has now been done. You can go further than 'keeping full notes' as the survey proceeds. You can write it up as you go along, in draft form. When done this way, 'writing up' is not a totally separate stage of the research, to be done only when other stages have been completed. On the contrary, keeping careful notes and writing drafts of the different stages on the way through the survey mean that writing is an integral part of the research process itself. 'Writing as you go' is a particularly useful strategy when the survey is also a dissertation.

With logical organisation and clear communication as the central aims of the survey report, I have written what follows with reference to the expectations and questions an experienced report reader will have in mind. I have called these the guiding questions. I suggest that you keep them in mind, as a guide, as you compile your survey report.

5.2 OBJECTIVES

Guiding questions: What was this survey about? What was it trying to find out? What were its research questions?

Here you can refer back directly to the objectives and research questions of your survey. They can be re-stated here, making use, as appropriate, of the hierarchy of abstraction from Chapter 3. A very good way to answer the first question in the reader's mind – what was this survey trying to find out? – is to state the general and specific research questions developed to guide the study. Just as they guided the study, they can now guide the way the report is written and the way it is read. Since, using the hierarchy of abstraction, the research questions are already at a more specific level of abstraction, it is also useful to repeat the more general statement of the objectives of the project before stating the research questions.

This fits in with the strategy of moving from the more general to the more specific, suggested later in this chapter as a technique for writing the introduction. Keep in mind that the above statement of your survey's objectives may become part of, or a sub-section of, a more general introduction, where the setting, context and background of your research are also described. If so, the hierarchy of abstraction gives a useful framework for organising and presenting your material in a way that is effective and easy to follow. But keep in mind also that a clear statement of your objectives and research questions remains central to the report, and that this statement should occur quite early in the document.

5.3 METHODS

Guiding questions: How was the survey done? What methods did it use?

Here, the reader's central interest is in the way the project was carried out. In a research environment, especially in a post-graduate research environment, readers need to be able to inspect the methods used in order to judge how much confidence to place in the survey's findings. It is convenient to subdivide this section into the headings used in Chapters 3 and 4, as shown below. Before the report deals with the detail of those sections, however, it is appropriate to describe briefly the overall logic and strategy of the survey in such terms as these:

> To answer these research questions, the overall strategy was to survey a sample of xxx students, selected to maximise variation in the independent variable(s), using a questionnaire partly developed for this project, and partly making use of existing measures. Data were summarised in terms of the main variables used in the research questions, and relationships between the variables were then studied.

This gives an overview of your methods and orients the reader immediately. It is also the sort of statement which can later go directly into your abstract (see section 5.5). The statements of overall strategy for the two examples are shown on pp. 80–1 and 90 in Chapter 6.

Conceptual framework

Guiding questions: What are the variables in this survey, and how are they seen in relation to each other? Which are the independent and dependent variables and, if appropriate, which are the context and control variables?

Here the conceptual framework developed earlier can be presented. A diagram will almost certainly be useful, and it should show the conceptual status of the variables in the study. Typically, this means showing the independent and dependent variables, and contextual, control and intervening variables, as appropriate. Chapter 6 shows the conceptual frameworks for both examples, as does Box 4.1 on p. 52.

Questionnaire

Guiding questions: How were the variables defined and measured? How was the questionnaire developed? Where can I see the items and questions?

The development of the questionnaire can be described here, including any pilot testing and the use of any existing instruments. This section may well have several sub-sections, dealing with the different variables and the different parts of the questionnaire. It is appropriate to show the final form of the questionnaire as an appendix to your report.

Sample

Guiding questions: What sample was selected for the study and why? What was the reasoning behind this selection? What limitations or biases might this sample have?

The report usually contains a written description which deals with these matters. It is also useful to show the sample in the form of a table, partitioned according to the main variables used in sample selection. Chapter 6 contains the description and sample diagrams for the two examples.

Data collection procedures

Guiding questions: What method of data collection was selected? How was access negotiated? What can be said about the quality of the data, including response rates?

Typically, a short description dealing with these matters is sufficient. Sometimes it is appropriate to show the sample of final respondents as a table, again partitioned by the main variables. However, tables in both this and the preceding section are probably not necessary, and the writer must judge which table would be more appropriate. If response rates are low, some comment is needed about the possible biases the responding sample (as against the selected sample) might show. Comments about the quality of data in this section are more impressionistic than technical. The question here is: How well did the data collection procedures work? Technical quality-of-data issues can come in the presentation of findings.

Data analysis procedures

Guiding questions: What methods and techniques were used to analyse the data?

At this point, and in view of the section on findings to follow, a short description of data analysis procedures is sufficient. For example:

> The internal consistency of subscales was examined using coefficient alpha; data on the main variables were summarised using means, standard deviations and frequency distributions; relationships between variables were investigated using correlation and regression techniques; differences between groups were examined using t tests and analysis of variance.

Note that, in this section, you are simply describing the data analysis methods used. The findings themselves are presented in the next section.

5.4 FINDINGS

Guiding questions: What did the survey find out? That is, what is the answer to each research question? What conclusions can be drawn from the findings?

Here is where the reporting is rather less straightforward and the writer faces more options. Presenting the findings of a survey can be quite complicated, and it is easy to lose the reader in a mass of detail, especially since statistics are involved in reporting the findings of a quantitative survey. Keeping the following two points in mind can help to overcome this problem.

First, the whole idea of the recommended data analysis approach is to simplify and summarise the complex set of initial data to reach findings and conclusions. The point is progressively to distil the pattern of relationships between the variables, and to express those relationships first in statistical terms and then in substantive terms which can be understood by non-technical readers. The analysis is directed first at obtaining scores for each person on each variable, secondly, at showing the distribution of each main variable, and thirdly at showing the relationships between the variables. Tables are important in summarising and presenting the results of the analysis.

Secondly, the framework provided by the research questions is a very good vehicle for presenting the findings. Since the research sets out to answer its research questions, and since this way of writing the report makes these questions central, the reader's question obviously is: What is the answer to each research question? The questions themselves have been developed in a logical way and relate to each other as specific research questions derived from more general research questions. Therefore, this way of presenting findings is by definition logical and easy for readers to follow. Of course, there may also be preliminary findings to present before the research questions themselves are answered – following the earlier framework, these would usually be about the psychometric characteristics of the measures used and the distribution of the variables across the sample. There may also be additional findings to report as a result of discoveries made during the analysis of the data. But the research questions themselves provide the main framework for the findings.

Thus, the recommended strategy for the main body of the findings is to take each specific research question, to present the statistical evidence and results relevant to that question, and to use this evidence to answer the question. Often, and especially if the research question is about the relationship between variables, the answer will be in two parts: one technical and one interpretive and substantive. For example:

'The data show a negative correlation between anxiety and achievement, which is statistically significant'.[2] This is a technical statement.

'The data show that higher scores on anxiety go with lower scores on achievement, which means that students who are more anxious score worse on these achievement measures'.[3] This is a substantive and interpretive statement.

The benefit of interpreting the technical statement substantively is that non-technical readers will get a better understanding of the survey's findings.

Findings versus conclusions

Sometimes the distinction between findings and conclusions is academic and hairsplitting. At other times it is important. The difference seems to lie in this question: How far does the researcher want to go beyond the data and the results which can clearly be seen in the data?

A *finding* is the answer to a specific research question – what the researcher found in answer to the question, or what the data clearly show. Sometimes that is the end of the matter, in which case the finding/conclusion distinction is academic – the finding is the conclusion.

At other times, however, the researcher wants to conclude something further on the basis of the finding(s). In this case, a *conclusion* is what the researcher concludes from the finding. It goes beyond the data; it is one step removed from the data. Here the distinction between finding and conclusion is important and linguistic care is required. Once again, the logical-links principle becomes important here. There needs to be a firm logical basis for moving from a finding to a conclusion.

There are two common ways of moving from findings to conclusions. One is abstracting or generalising, going from the more specific statement of the finding to the more general statement of the conclusion.[4] The other refers back to the structure of general and specific research questions highlighted earlier. Since a general research question leads to several specific research questions, the answers to the specific research questions can be grouped together to form an answer to the general research question. This then becomes a conclusion. By definition, it is at a more abstract and general level. Thus the two ways, which appear different, are essentially the same.

While the essence of the survey report is contained in these three sections – objectives, methods and findings – in many situations the report will need other sections as well. The next section focuses on the survey report as a post-graduate dissertation. In this case, a number of other sections are needed to fill out the report, and they are listed and briefly described below. If you are not a graduate student writing a dissertation, you will have to judge which of the following sections are appropriate for the audience for your survey report.

5.5 CHECKLIST OF SECTION HEADINGS

When the survey report is also a dissertation, the additional sections needed are the abstract, introduction, literature review, discussion, references and appendices. This leads to the full list of section headings shown in Table 5.1.

These additional sections are now briefly discussed. More information on them is also given in *Introduction to Social Research* (Punch, 1998: Chapter 12) and in *Developing Effective Research Proposals* (Punch, 2000: Chapter 6).

TABLE 5.1 *Checklist of section headings for the survey report*

Abstract
Introduction – background, context, setting
Objectives and research questions
Literature review
Methods – overall strategy
– conceptual framework
– questionnaire
– sample
– data collection
– data analysis
Findings
Discussion
References
Appendices

Abstract

The abstract is a brief summary of the finished study. For a quantitative-survey-relating-variables, it should have three parts, summarising respectively the objectives, methods and findings. Writing the abstract involves using and summarising what has already been written. A good abstract need only occupy 100 words or less, and is written last.

Introduction

The essential purpose of the introduction is to locate the study in its broader context and to describe its setting and any necessary background. While there are many ways to introduce any topic, a good general strategy is to work from the general to the specific. The hierarchy of concepts described earlier, especially the area-topic-general-research-question part of it, is useful here. It is also important to give the reader, as early as possible, a clear statement of the survey's objectives and research questions. It is a matter of judgement for the writer whether that statement forms part of the introduction or a separate section, as suggested in Table 5.1.

Literature review

In a post-graduate dissertation, the literature review is especially important. Its function is to locate the present study in relation to the relevant literature and to show how it contributes to that literature. It normally constitutes a separate chapter in a dissertation which is a survey, and also provides themes for the consideration and interpretation of this survey's findings in the later discussion section of the report. In addition to the references given at the start of this section, Hart has written valuable books on reviewing the literature (Hart, 1998) and on searching the literature (Hart, 2001).

Discussion

The discussion section is where the writer considers the findings and conclusions of the survey in a broader context, having thoroughly reported earlier on the survey's objectives, methods and findings. As with the introduction, there are many ways to do this, but this is the one place in the report where you as the writer can say what you think the findings mean, and perhaps also what should be done in the light of them. This takes the discussion towards implications and recommendations and these words may also be included in the section heading. If the discussion does lead to a consideration of the implications of the findings, a useful three-part framework is:

- implications for theory;
- implications for practice;
- implications for further research.

It is also useful – and usually expected in a dissertation – that discussion of the findings will refer back to the themes identified earlier in the literature review.

References

All references cited in the report should be listed in appropriate scholarly format in the reference list.

Appendices

Any additional material can be included as appendices to the report. The questionnaire and covering letters will usually constitute one appendix. Detailed statistical tables often constitute another appendix. They are there for the reader to consult if desired, but are judged by the writer to be not essential, or too detailed, to include in the body of the report.

Regarding the order of sections, there is no formula for the 'correct' order of the sections in the report. There is, however, a very good rule to follow: make sure the order of sections is logical so that it is easy for the reader to follow. In other words, organise for understanding. With that rule in mind, the order of sections shown in Table 5.1 is generally recommended.[5] The objectives, methods and findings sections are the heart of the report, but other sections are also important in presenting a complete and well-rounded dissertation.

5.6 REVIEW CONCEPTS AND QUESTIONS

survey report

objectives
What was this survey about? What was it trying to find out? What were its research questions?

methods
How was the survey done? What methods did it use?
overall strategy

conceptual framework
What are the variables in this survey, and how are they seen in relation to each other? Which are the independent and dependent variables and, if appropriate, which are the context and control variables?

questionnaire
How were the variables defined and measured? How was the questionnaire developed?
Where can I see the items and questions?

sample
What sample was selected for the study and why? What was the reasoning behind this selection? What limitations or biases might this sample have?

Data collection procedures
What method of data collection was selected? How was access negotiated? What can be said about the quality of the data, including response rates?

data analysis procedures
What methods and techniques were used to analyse the data?

findings
What did the survey find out? That is, what is the answer to each research question? What conclusions can be drawn from the finding?

abstract
introduction – background, context, setting, purpose
literature review
discussion
references
appendices

NOTES

1. Throughout the book, I have used the term 'objectives'. Sometimes these are called purposes or aims. Similarly, I use the term 'findings'. Sometimes these are called results. The term 'conclusions', on the other hand, means something slightly different from the findings, as is discussed in section 5.4 in this chapter.

2. 'Statistical significance' is a technical term which involves the validity of inferences from a sample to a population. It deals with the question: How likely is it that what was found to be true for the sample is also true of the population from which the sample was drawn? (See Chapter 3.) The answer is expressed as the probability of being wrong in making such an inference. Thus $p<.05$ means that I will be wrong less than 5 times in 100 if I infer that what I found in my sample is also true of my population. By convention, probability levels of less than .05 are accepted as statistically significant. See Appendix 1 for further reading on statistical significance.

3. The overall objective of a quantitative survey is to arrive at substantive conclusions about the way the variables are related to each other. The conclusions need to be firmly based on technical foundations, but they also, in the end, need to be substantive, both because there will be non-technical readers of the survey report and because building substantive knowledge is the objective of the research. In my opinion, quantitative survey data analysis is sometimes presented in terms that are too technical, and insufficiently substantive and interpretive.

4. Referring to statistical significance in note 2 above, we could also say that the sample result is the finding and the population inference is

the conclusion. However, that is not the distinction I am making here.

5. It is sometimes recommended that the literature review comes before the research questions. If this is done, the 'objectives and research questions' section can be split into two, with objectives coming before the literature review and research questions after.

6

Examples

CONTENTS

6.1 INTRODUCTION

This chapter contains the examples referred to in earlier chapters. Following the logic of this book – to describe the simple model of the quantitative survey first, then to show how it generalises to more complex examples – the two examples are related. The first is simple, with two independent variables and one dependent variable. The second, an extension of the first, is more complex, with context and control variables added.

Both versions come from educational research, but the method illustrated here applies just as well to other areas. The examples are presented here not as the report of a finished project, but use the headings and sections of earlier chapters in order to illustrate the points made and to show how the project develops. There is discussion throughout the chapter of the points made in earlier chapters.

6.2 SIMPLE EXAMPLE

This small-scale quantitative survey investigates the relationship between mental ability (MA) and time on task (TT) as independent variables and school achievement as dependent variable. Its strategy is to measure a sample of secondary school students on MA, TT and school achievement, and to use these measures to study the relationships between the variables. It is now presented in terms of the headings of earlier chapters.

Area, topic and research questions

Using the hierarchy of concepts in Chapter 3, this project can be set up as follows:

Area   Students' achievement at school
Topic   Determinants of scholastic achievement

General research question

What is the relationship between MA and TT as independent variables and school achievement as dependent variable?

This question also serves to describe the objective of this survey. Clearly, the overall objective is to study the relationship between MA, TT and school achievement.

Specific research questions

The above general research question subdivides naturally into four specific research questions:

1   What is the relationship between MA and school achievement?
2   What is the relationship between TT and school achievement?
3   What is the relationship between MA and TT?
4   What is the joint relationship between MA, TT and school achievement?

This subdivision follows a straightforward and recurrent pattern. In the first two questions, we look at the separate or bivariate relationships between the independent variables and dependent variable. In the fourth question, we look at the joint or multi-variable relationship between the independent variables and dependent variables. In the third question, (3) above, we look at the relationship between the two independent variables. Even though this is not the main focus of the project, we should take advantage of this data set to see how MA and TT relate. It is clearly a question of interest.

The hierarchy of concepts – from more general to more specific

We can see the hierarchy, from more general to more specific, in this set-up. Thus, the topic (determinants of school achievement) is more specific than the research area (students' achievement at school). That is, determinants of school achievement give more focus to the survey than the general statement of students' achievement at school. The general research question makes matters more specific again. From the many possible determinants of school achievement, the general research question identifies MA and TT.[1] The specific research questions go further and split the general question into its components parts.

As noted in Chapter 5 (section 5.2, pp. 69–70), this hierarchy of concepts can be very helpful when writing the introduction section of the report. A good way – one that is logical, easy to write and easy for the reader to follow – is to introduce the project first at its most general level, then to move to more specific levels and questions. Having the more general statements first also usually makes it easier to show the context around the research.

The empirical criterion

Does each specific research question above meet the empirical criterion? Is it clear what information each question requires? To answer the first specific research question, we need to measure the MA and achievement level of each student. To answer the second, we need to measure the TT and achievement level of each student. The third and fourth questions require the same information. Thus each question meets the criterion and we can easily see the list of variables required – MA, TT, achievement.

Conceptual framework

This project has a simple conceptual framework, with two independent variables and one dependent variable. It is shown below.

Independent variables   **Dependent variable**

Mental Ability MA ⎫
                  ⎬ ⟶ Achievement
Time on Task TT ⎭

We should note again that this is not the only conceptual framework possible with these variables.[2] Thus even a small number of variables gives multiple possibilities as to how a study might be set up. There is no one right or correct choice among these possibilities. It is up to the researcher to choose among them and to decide the set-up – that is, the conceptual framework and the research questions – for the project. It is important to consider the various possibilities, to choose among them on some logical basis, to make the set-up clear, and to make other parts of the study fit together around the chosen set-up.

Strategy

A sample of secondary school students will be measured with respect to MA, TT and achievement levels, and the relationships between the variables will then be studied, first individually, then jointly. Sampling decisions will be required, as will decisions on how to measure the variables. Clearly, in this case the individual student is the unit of analysis.

The questionnaire

Development of the questionnaire starts by asking what data are required. The research questions clearly indicate the data required in this project. The variables to be measured are MA, TT and achievement level.

Mental ability – MA

The term intelligence is usually associated with the whole range of human capabilities. Because of that, and because of the focus of this research, the term 'mental ability' is restricted here to students to include students' verbal and number abilities only. A variety of measures, often developed in different countries, exist to measure such concepts. In the Australian context, for example, the Australian Council for Educational Research has developed, standardised and normed a test of verbal reasoning and a corresponding test of number reasoning. These tests produce two scores which can be used separately or combined into a composite score to represent overall mental ability. An advantage of using these measures is that schools often administer such tests as part of normal operations.[3]

The measurement of such concepts as mental ability is also a sensitive issue so the researcher wishing to measure MA must tread carefully and ethically. For the purposes of this example, we will assume that the schools involved already have the measures of MA noted above, and have agreed to make these available under suitable ethical arrangements for research purposes. Fortunately, this can sometimes happen for the lucky educational researcher.

Time on task – TT

Conceptual definition: This variable measures how much out-of-class time a student spends doing homework, studying and doing study-related activities.

Here the situation is different from the other two variables in this research. While time on tasks has been investigated in research, standardised measures do not exist, and different researchers have constructed their own measure of the variable.

To do the same here, a set of draft items for self-report by students on a self-administered questionnaire would be developed and pre-tested with a sample of secondary school students. The items would ask students, in various ways, to report how much time they spend doing specific homework and study-related activities. Pre-test analysis would enable the selection of a final set of, say, 12 items, each with a four-point Likert scale response, and each scored so that 1 represents little time and 4 represents a lot of time. This would produce aggregate scale scores for this variable with a possible range from 12 (12×1, very little time spent) to 48 (12×4, a great deal of time spent).

Achievement

As with MA, it is not realistic for the researcher to think of constructing school achievement measures for research purposes – certainly not the dissertation researcher. Measuring school achievement is a very complex area – made even more so at the secondary school level because of different school subjects – and, like mental ability, it is an area where enormous effort has been invested over a long period of time. In addition, of course, schools already do take regular measures of school achievement. Therefore, the only sensible thing here is for the researcher to try to negotiate access to already existing school achievement data.

At upper secondary school level, schools often take achievement measures across different subjects and then combine them into an overall achievement score. We will assume that access to these scores can be negotiated with this project so that achievement is measured uni-dimensionally.[4]

Thus the survey questionnaire for this example is very short. It includes the items to measure TT and background information to enable other data to be matched with the questionnaire data. The other data, on MA and achievement, are to be obtained from school records. The covering letter for the questionnaire also needs only to be short and to include instructions for completing the questionnaire.

The sample

Following the logic stressed in Chapters 3 and 4, an ideal sample for this study would be one which shows good variability in both independent variables, MA and TT. It is difficult to see how variability in TT can be structured into the sample since there is little prior knowledge about the way this variable is distributed. Therefore it is important to try to ensure variability in this variable through sensitivity in question development and in the way the variable is measured.

Achieving sample variability in MA is in some ways easier. Some secondary schools admit students on the basis of superior performance on some sort of entrance examination. In such 'elite' schools, it is likely that variability in MA among students is relatively restricted. This is surely the case if MA itself is used in the entrance examination. In other cases, schools take in a much wider cross-section of students. Reasonable variation in MA is much more likely in such 'comprehensive' schools. For this example, therefore, we will aim to sample students from comprehensive secondary schools.

This highlights a recurrent sampling issue for educational research, and for other settings where the individual is the unit of analysis, but where individuals are grouped.[5] The individual student is the unit of analysis, but in education systems students are grouped into classes, and classes into schools. One sampling strategy would be to ignore this structure and to draw students from a number of schools without reference to class designation. Such a strategy is, however, both inefficient and idealistic – if nothing else, a graduate student's resources would probably not permit it. Therefore a better strategy is to use the structure and to sample intact classes from selected schools.

Two other variables, or sampling parameters, need consideration in the sampling for this project. One is age, the other is gender. They are not included as variables in the conceptual framework and research questions, although they could easily be. But they soon emerge as important variables, especially age, when we think about the sample in its school setting.

Secondary schools typically take students from 12 to 17 years of age. We will have to decide whether to sample across all of these ages or whether to control on age by selecting only one age band.[6] The former decision – to sample across all ages – will substantially increase the size of sample required. This is because, as noted in Chapter 4, the more variables in the design, the larger the sample size required, and dealing with age this way is including age in the design. The latter decision – selecting only one age band – is therefore more practical and realistic, especially in a small project. Given that, a decision is then required as to which age band to choose. Following the idea of giving a relationship the maximum chance to be observed, it makes sense to take 16 year olds since there are grounds for thinking that both MA and TT take on more importance as upper secondary school work becomes more academically demanding.

Regarding gender, similar reasoning could be applied. The sample could be restricted to either boys or girls. But with only two gender categories, and with many comprehensive schools co-educational, it is better not to restrict the generalisability of the study and to let gender vary. Thus we will not control gender in the sample design, but let it vary. As long as we have approximately equal numbers of boys and girls, we can investigate the role of gender in the relationships identified in the research questions.

We will assume that class size is approximately 30, that three comprehensive schools have agreed to take part, each having two classes of 16 year olds with approximately equal numbers of boys and girls. The schools themselves are selected on the basis of being comprehensive schools, being willing to take part in the research, being willing to make MA and achievement data available, and being willing to assist by providing class time for the collection of other data.

This sampling plan is shown in Table 6.1.

Data collection

Considering the situation here, and the data collection alternatives, the preferred decision is for the researcher to administer the questionnaire face to face to intact groups of students, taking advantage of the school situation. This is one of the advantages of educational research in those cases where school cooperation can be obtained. It results in a response rate of virtually 100%. The questionnaires are then proofread and the data entered into the computer for analysis.

Data analysis

The data analysis follows the steps laid out in Chapter 4 (pp. 63–5). The first two of the six steps described there have already been done (proofreading and data entry), so the four main steps now are the psychometric analysis, descriptive summaries, bivariate relationships and multi-variable relationships.

TABLE 6.1   *Sampling plan*

School	Classes		Totals
	1	2	
1	30*	30	60
2	30	30	60
3	30	30	60
Total			180

* Class numbers are approximate

Psychometric analysis

As noted, there are two objectives of this stage. The first is to ensure the best possible measurements of the variables, with reference both to variation between people and to internal consistency for multiple-item scales. The second is to create scores on each variable for each person. Until this is done we are working with item scores for each person. After this stage, item scores are left behind,[7] and the subsequent analysis concentrates on variable or scale scores.

In this example, we do not have much analysis to do at this stage, since we are working with already existing measures on two of the three variables. We can assume that the measures of both mental ability and achievement have satisfactory psychometric properties since they come from well-established instruments.

The measure of TT was developed for this project. It was a 12-item scale, designed to produce one score. Each item is scored 1 to 4, so that total scores range from 12 to 48, with higher scores representing more TT and lower scores less TT. In the interests of working with the best possible scale scores, we would examine the extent to which each item produced variation (for this we can use standard deviations and frequency distributions), the correlations between the items and, based on the inter-item correlations, the extent of internal consistency as measured by coefficient alpha. On the basis of this analysis, assume that two items are rejected, both producing relatively little variation and both correlating poorly with the remaining 10 items. The final score for TT is thus based on 10 items, with possible scale scores ranging from 10 to 40, and coefficient alpha for this 10-item scale above 0.8.

When this stage of the analysis has been completed, the data set has been very substantially reduced and consolidated. We have now summarised the data into three overall scores for each student, one score representing each of the variables MA, TT and achievement.

Summarising the data – distribution of variables

Before proceeding with the distribution of variables, we should consider a data analysis issue which arises because of the sampling structure we

TABLE 6.2 *Distribution of variables*

	Mean	Standard deviation	Score range
MA (N = 180)			
TT (N = 180)			
Achievement (N = 180)			

have used – classes and schools. In the analysis, we would like to 'pool' the data, ignoring the fact that scores come from different classes and schools. We would like to do that because it will make the analysis simpler and easier to follow. Strictly speaking, then, we should check that there are not systematic differences between classes and schools before pooling the scores. We can do that using one-way analysis of variance (see Appendix 1), comparing scores on each of the three variables across classes and schools, and testing for statistical significance of differences between them. We would also do that with gender groups before pooling the data. In this case, with only two categories, one-way analysis of variance reduces to the t test.

Assuming that no systematic differences exist between these groups, we would proceed to pool data by ignoring the class and school 'locations' of each student, and gender, from this point on in the analysis. Before investigating relationships between the variables, we want to know how each is distributed across this sample. To do this, we can use both means and standard deviations, and frequency distributions. The frequency distributions give us a very detailed picture of the way the variable is distributed, whereas the mean and standard deviation summarise the distribution. Both are useful, but it is usual to show the means and standard deviations in the text of the report, and frequency distributions in the appendices.[8] We would draw up a summary table to report the distribution results from this stage of the analysis (see Table 6.2 for the general form of this table).

Bivariate relationships

After the preliminary analysis of the above two stages, we are now guided by the research questions, in this stage by questions (1), (2) and (3) – see p. 81. With each main variable now in continuous variable form, we can use Pearson product-moment correlation (r) and summarise the results in a table, such as that shown in Table 6.3.

This stage of the analysis, as well as answering the research questions, helps us to understand how each variable relates to each other variable. At this point, we are examining the overall relationship of one variable with another, without taking into consideration any third variable.[9]

TABLE 6.3 *Correlations between variables*

	MA	TT	Achievement
MA	1.00		
TT		1.00	
Achievement			1.00

With N = 180, r = .15, p < .05. This means that, with a sample size of 180, a correlation coefficient of numerical value greater than or equal to 0.15 is required to reach statistical significance at the 5% level. See also Chapter 5, note 2 (p. 78).

Multi-variable relationships[10]

Here we refer to research question (4) – p. 81. With two continuous independent variables, we can use multiple linear regression to study the joint relationships between the two independent variables and the dependent variable. Chapter 7 gives details about how multiple linear regression analysis works. From this analysis, we derive two main statistics. The first is R^2, the squared multiple correlation coefficient, which tells us how much of the variance in the dependent variable is accounted for by the independent variables. The second is the partial standardised regression weight, called beta weight (β), which tells us how much change in the dependent variable is produced by a change in each independent variable – that is, these weights tell us how important each independent variable is in predicting the dependent variable.

Both statistics are valuable. The squared multiple correlation coefficient, which can vary between 0 and 1.0, gives us a picture of how much of the variance in the dependent variable we can account for or explain. For example, if $R^2=0.7$, we know that about 70% of the variance is accounted for, and we are well on the way to understanding the dependent variable. If $R^2=0.1$, on the other hand, we can only account for about 10% of the variance. The majority of its variance, some 90%, is unaccounted for by these independent variables, and we have to look elsewhere to understand it.

The regression weights, which (in standardised form) also vary between 0 and 1.0, tell us which of the independent variables exert the main influence on the dependent variable. A beta weight of 0.05, for example, tells us that changing this independent variable will not affect the dependent variable very much – this independent variable is not very important. A beta weight of say 0.45, on the other hand, tells us that changing this independent variable will affect the dependent variable substantially – this independent variable is much more important. As with correlation coefficients, the sign of the beta weight tells us the direction of the relationship between that independent variable and the dependent variable.

TABLE 6.4 *Regression analysis results (dependent variable achievement)*

Independent variables	β weight	Significance
MA		
TT		
$R^2 = \ldots p <$		

Thus the results of the regression analysis would be summarised in a table such as that shown in Table 6.4.

This completes the data analysis for this project. Each research question can now be answered, in both technical and substantive language. The report for this project is now straightforward to organise, along the lines described in Chapter 5.

6.3   COMPLEX EXAMPLE

This extended and more complex example builds on the simple one, adding social class (SES)[11] as a context variable and student alienation from school as a control variable around it. Thus this more complex small-scale quantitative survey investigates the relationship between MA and TT as independent variables and achievement as dependent variable, after having controlled the effect of alienation and within differing social class (SES) contexts. Its strategy is more complex than before, but is based on the same logic – to measure a sample of secondary school students on MA, TT, school achievement, alienation and SES, and to use these measures to study the relationships between the variables according to the conceptual framework and research questions.

Essentially, two things are more complex here: the conceptual framework and the research questions. They lead in turn to a longer questionnaire (with a more complex conceptual map behind it) and to a more complex task in the data analysis, and especially in its write-up. But this is clearly still a quantitative survey of the type described in this book and with the same basic logic.

The extended example will be described in terms of the earlier headings. Before that, two terms need clarification:

- Context variable: As I am using the term here, this means a variable which provides a context for another relationship between variables. Thus, to say that SES is a context variable is to say we will investi-

gate how another relationship – for example that between MA and achievement – varies across different levels of SES.
- Control variable: As used here, this means a variable whose effects will be controlled or removed. To use alienation level as a control variable is to remove its effects from achievement (the dependent variable) in order to see how the independent variables relate to achievement with the effects of alienation removed.

Area, topic and research questions

The area and topic remain, as before in the simple example (see p. 81), but the general and specific research questions now need to be expanded and rephrased.

General research questions

1 What is the relationship between MA and TT as independent variables and school achievement as dependent variable, after controlling for the effect of student alienation from school?
2 How does this relationship vary for different levels of SES?

Bringing these two questions together gives us a summary statement of the objective of the project – to study the effect of MA and TT on achievement, after controlling for alienation and in the context of differing SES levels.

Specific research questions

The first general research question subdivides as follows:

1 What is the relationship between MA and school achievement?
2 What is the relationship between TT and school achievement?
3 What is the relationship between alienation and school achievement?
4 What is the joint relationship between MA, TT and school achievement after controlling for alienation?

The second general research question subdivides as follows:

5 What is the relationship between SES and each of MA, TT, alienation and school achievement?[12]

6 How does the joint relationship between MA, TT and school achievement vary across different levels of SES, after controlling for alienation?

The earlier comments about the hierarchy of concepts apply here (p. 82), as do those about the empirical criterion (p. 82). Each specific research question clearly meets the empirical criterion and the variable list is now five – MA, TT, achievement, SES and alienation.

Conceptual framework

The conceptual framework for the survey is now more complex. With SES as a context variable and alienation as a control variable, we can show it as:

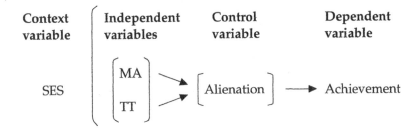

The questionnaire

We have now added the two variables SES and alienation to the list of variables which need to be measured. Unlike MA and achievement, the measures for these cannot be obtained from already existing school records.

Socio-economic status (SES)

This variable has been extensively studied, and measured, both in sociological and educational research. In a study such as this, with SES as a context variable, it is sufficient to have a three-level classification – upper, middle, lower. It is sometimes measured by a composite of the educational levels and the occupational status of parents. Since these are usually highly correlated, a simpler but effective measure is the occupational status of the main breadwinner. For occupational status, a detailed way to measure is to ask respondents to provide both a title for the job or position and a brief description of the type and level of work, and then to refer this information to the occupational prestige rating scales for the country in question. This leads to a scale score for SES (with the number of points on the scale varying between different countries). These scale scores can then be used to derive the three-level classification – upper, middle and lower.

Alienation level

This variable has been well studied in educational research and different measures have been developed. After reviewing existing scales, the choice here is a modified form of the Bardsley (1976) alienation scale, with 15 items covering the three most relevant dimensions of alienation, and combined into a single-scale score. This scale has been shown to have high internal consistency (alpha = .90). It is a Likert summated rating scale with each item scored 1 (low alienation) to 4 (high alienation). Thus, total scores can range from 15 (15×1, very low alienation) to 60 (15×4, very high alienation).

Thus the final form of the questionnaire for this example includes, in addition to background information, the 12 items to measure TT, as before, but also the 15 items to measure alienation and those to measure SES. The covering letter for the questionnaire would be similar to the earlier one.

The sample

Because there are now five variables, the sample needs to be bigger than the previous sample and, in addition to earlier considerations, it needs to show variability in SES – specific research question (6) cannot be answered without variation in SES. A sample size of approximately 350 would be adequate for a project of this scope. This requires six schools.

To ensure SES variability, we could use either of two strategies in selecting the six schools:

- ensure two schools are from upper SES catchment areas, two are from middle SES areas and two are from lower SES areas; or
- ensure all six schools draw their students from across the SES range. With comprehensive schools this is possible.

Practicalities and questions of access would, of course, be of overriding importance in this matter. If there is a choice, the second is a better strategy to follow. In the first, there is the possibility of school effects being 'block booked' with SES levels.[13]

The earlier comments (p. 85) about age and gender apply, and we can assume here the same decisions as earlier – the sample will be restricted

TABLE 6.5   *Sampling plan*

School	Classes		Totals
	1	2	
1	30*	30	60
2	30	30	60
3	30	30	60
4	30	30	60
5	30	30	60
6	30	30	60
Total			360

* As before, class numbers are approximate

to 16 year olds and will include both boys and girls. Thus the sampling plan is as shown in Table 6.5.

Data collection

Again, earlier comments apply (p. 86), but the questionnaire is now longer and we need to ensure, through pilot testing, that students can answer the question about the occupation of the main breadwinner. We will assume, as before, that the cooperation of school authorities enables us to administer questionnaires to intact classes, again with a response rate of virtually 100%.

Data analysis

This is now described in some detail again since, in my experience, this is where beginning research students have most difficulty.

We begin, as always, with the proofreading of answered questionnaires and data entry. After that, and as before, the four main stages are the psychometric analysis, descriptive summaries, bivariate relationships and multi-variable relationships.

Psychometric analysis

The 15-item alienation scale should be checked for its basic psychometric properties, especially the extent to which items discriminate between people, the correlations between items and thus the internal consistency of the scale. As before, it may be that some items are rejected at this stage and the scale shortened. But, since it is an established measure, we will assume that all items discriminate and correlate well, and that internal consistency is satisfactory. Thus the scale remains at 15 items,

TABLE 6.6 *Distribution of variables*

	Mean	Standard deviation	Score range
SES			
MA			
TT			
Alienation			
Achievement			

with possible scale scores ranging from 15 to 60. The TT measure would be analysed along similar lines as before (p. 87), and we can assume the same conclusion: 12 items are reduced to 10, scale scores range from 10 to 40 and coefficient alpha is above 0.8. The SES measure does not need any internal consistency analysis since it is a single item.

As before, the data set is now reduced and consolidated. We have one scale score for each of TT and alienation, instead of the original 12 items and 15 items respectively, and one score for SES. Overall, we now have five scores for each individual, one each for MA, TT, achievement, alienation and SES. We also know the gender and class and school location for each student. This reduced data set becomes the basis for subsequent analysis.

Summarising the data – distribution of variables
We extend this stage of the analysis reported for the simple example to include the distribution of SES and alienation. Again, we can use mainly means and standard deviations, supplemented as required by frequency distributions. We can display the results as shown in Table 6.6.

Again, we check that there are no systematic differences between classes, schools and gender groups on SES and alienation, and then we proceed to work with the pooled data.

Bivariate relationships
Before focusing on the bivariate research questions (1), (2), (3) and (5), it is a good idea to compute and report bivariate relationships between all variables in one consolidated table. In this extended example, the table would appear as that shown in Table 6.7.

We can now extract the relevant information from this table to answer directly research questions (1), (2), (3) and (5) – see p. 91. In addition, Table 6.7 also tells us how the context variable SES and the control variable alienation relate to the independent and dependent variables (see also Appendix 2 for the outline of a survey project investigating the relationship between SES and alienation).

TABLE 6.7 *Correlations between variables*

	SES	MA	TT	Alienation	Achievement
SES	1.00				
MA		1.00			
TT			1.00		
Alienation				1.00	
Achievement					1.00

With N = 360, r = .11, p < .05

Multi-variable relationships

The focus now is on specific research questions (4) and (6). I will work through them in some detail.

Research question (4): *What is the joint relationship between MA, TT and school achievement after controlling for alienation?*
  To answer this, we use stepwise regression (a variant of multiple linear regression – see Chapter 7, p. 107), with alienation as the covariate or control variable. To do this, we compute two regression equations.

- For the first, we use alienation alone to predict achievement. The R^2 for this model tells us how much of the variance in achievement is associated with, or accounted for by, alienation.
- For the second, we use MA, TT and alienation to predict achievement. The R^2 for this model tells us how much of the variance in achievement is accounted for by these three variables.

The difference between the two R^2s tells us the effect of MA and TT on achievement over and above the effect of alienation on achievement.[14]
  It is worth describing the logic of this procedure in some detail. The research question, as stated earlier, is:

- *What is the joint relationship between MA, TT and school achievement after controlling for alienation?*

In statistical-operational terms, this question really means:

- *How much of the variance in achievement is associated with variance in MA and TT, after the variance in achievement associated with alienation has been removed?*

Thus, after taking out the variance in achievement associated with alienation, we examine how much of the remaining variance in achievement is associated with MA and TT. This is what it means to ask 'What

TABLE 6.8 *Regression analysis results (dependent variable achievement)*

Model 1	Beta	R^2
Predictor variable		
Alienation		
		$(F= \ldots, p = \ldots)$

Model 2	Beta	R^2
Predictor variables		
Alienation		
MA		
TT		
		$(F= \ldots, p = \ldots)$

Model 1 vs Model 2	$F = \ldots, p = \ldots$	

is the relationship between MA, TT and achievement after controlling for alienation?' Sometimes the phrase 'after controlling for' is replaced by the phrase 'having removed the effects of'. As this description shows, the two phrases mean the same thing. The technical name for this is analysis of covariance, and this description shows, logically, how the technique is carried out using regression analysis.

We can summarise these regression results in a table, as shown in Table 6.8.

Research question (6): *How does the joint relationship between MA, TT and school achievement vary across different levels of SES, after controlling for alienation?*

There are different ways we could answer this question, but the simplest is to re-compute the two steps for research question (6) within each SES level. That is, we partition the sample according to the three SES levels. We then re-compute the regression analysis models described above. That is, within each SES level:

- first, we use alienation to predict achievement, and compute the R^2;
- second, we use alienation, MA and TT to predict achievement and compute the R^2;
- then we test the significance of the difference between the two R^2s.

Doing this three times gives us three sets of results which tell us how the relationship varies in the context of SES. These results can be presented in a table having the form of Table 6.8 above, but having three partitions within it, one for each SES level.

With all research questions answered, we can now proceed to the report of the survey, again following the guidelines of Chapter 5.

NOTES

1. There should be good reason for the selection of these two determinants, and a dissertation would need to justify their selection.
2. Another possibility is to have MA as a control variable and to look at the relationship between TT and performance having controlled on MA. The conceptual framework for that is:

Independent variable	Control variable	Dependent variable

$$TT \longrightarrow \left[MA \right] \longrightarrow \text{Achievement}$$

Still another possibility is to control on TT and to look at the relationship between MA and achievement with TT controlled. The conceptual framework here is:

Independent variable	Control variable	Dependent variable

$$MA \longrightarrow \left[TT \right] \longrightarrow \text{Achievement}$$

3. I am grateful to Barry Sheridan for pointing this out. It was originally discussed in his masters thesis (Sheridan, 1976).
4. An interesting complication arises here for the variables mental ability and school achievement. For simplicity in this example, both are assumed to be scored as uni-dimensional variables. Both are also, in their primary form, multi-dimensional variables. Thus, mental ability has two primary scores and achievement has numerous primary scores, depending on the number of school subjects measured. The analysis can proceed with both variables in primary form. For mental ability, the complication is not great – instead of two independent variables we have three. For achievement, the complication is more significant – we now have multiple correlated dependent variables, technically requiring multi-variate rather than uni-variate statistical analysis.
5. Organisational studies are often another example of this sampling issue.

6. This is only one form of control. See *Introduction to Social Research*, Chapter 7 (Punch, 1998: 83–5).
7. They are 'left behind', but of course retained and not destroyed. They can be returned to for more detailed analysis, if necessary.
8. More detailed tables, for example showing the above statistics for individual schools and classes, or showing frequency distributions, can be placed in the appendix to the report.
9. Correlation coefficients vary numerically between 0 and ±1.00, with the sign indicating the direction of the relationship and the numerical value indicating its strength. The coefficient summarises the relationship between the two variables. Note that the correlation matrix shown in Table 6.2 is diagonal – thus, the correlation between MA and TT is the same as that between TT and MA, and so on.
10. I have used the awkward term 'multi-variable' to indicate many variables rather than the term 'multi-variate'. This latter term has a specialised technical meaning. It means multiple *dependent* variables.
11. The variable commonly known as social class is usually called *Socio-Economic Status* in research and is abbreviated to SES.
12. As an additional example, a quantitative survey to study the relationship between SES and alienation is outlined in Appendix 2. For illustration, it is presented there as a separate survey. It could, of course, be a sub-project of this survey.
13. Variables are said to be 'block booked' when partitioning a sample according to one variable is also, at the same time, partitioning it on one or more other variables. In such cases it becomes difficult to know which of the block booked variables is having any observed effect on the dependent variable. Thus, in the first alternative suggested, SES might be block booked with ethnicity (see Rosenberg, 1968).
14. The difference between the two R^2s can be tested for statistical significance using the F test (see Kerlinger and Pedhazur, 1973; Allison, 1999).

7

Generalising the Simple Model

CONTENTS

7.1 INTRODUCTION

This book is based on the premise that the quantitative-survey-relating-variables is a central strategy for inquiry in quantitative research, and therefore an essential part of the training of researchers in social science. The book has taken a simple version of such a survey, pulled it apart to see its essential elements, described each element to show how it works, and illustrated it with a detailed example, first in simple form, then in more complex form. Several times in earlier chapters it has been stressed that the technique generalises to more complex situations. This chapter shows two of the more common generalisations.

Chapters 1 and 2 have also stressed that the quantitative-survey-relating-variables is the basis for non-experimental quantitative methods in social science research. These methods have assumed steadily greater importance as social science research has become more and more widely applied. From the research training point of view, therefore, a thorough grounding in the methods of the quantitative survey, starting with the simple version and basic strategy and then generalising it, is desirable.

The basic strategy of the type of quantitative survey dealt with in this book can, once again, be briefly summarised:

Once the objectives and research questions for a survey are clear, they tell us what the unit of analysis is (most commonly it is the individual person), what the variables are and what the conceptual framework is which ties the variables together. We then work out how to measure a sample of people on the variables indicated, and proceed to study the relationships between the variables according to the research questions and the conceptual framework.

It is this strategy which generalises to more complex situations. What 'more complex situations' really means is more variables, more complex conceptual frameworks among the variables, and therefore more complex sets of research questions. The most common, and widely applicable, of these generalisations takes two main forms, presented now as sections 7.2 and 7.3. The first shows multiple independent variables, the second shows control variables. An example of the second was given in the extended example of Chapter 6. After that, the chapter then has a section on multiple linear regression analysis as a general design and data analysis framework for conducting such projects (see section 7.4).

7.2 MULTIPLE INDEPENDENT VARIABLES

The most straightforward extension of the simple quantitative survey involves multiple independent variables and one dependent variable. Thus the simple example in Chapter 6 has two independent variables, and surveys with three or more independent variables are common. While there is conceptually no limit to the number of independent variables we can use, there are certainly limits imposed by common sense, practical considerations and sample size.

Common sense and practical limitations tell us not to overload a particular survey, just because the logic generalises. Sample size imposes limits because adding more and more variables dramatically increases the sample size required for a project to be viable.[1] The implication is that we should think carefully about each independent variable we add to the survey.

There is another reason for thinking carefully about both the number and nature of independent variables we add. This is often described under the technical term of *multicollinearity*. This term refers to the degree of correlation between independent variables (Allison, 1999: 62–4). On a common-sense level, it means independent variables which overlap with each other and which therefore do not contribute additional or unique variance to the dependent variable. While some degree of correlation between independent variables is acceptable (and, indeed, is necessary for MLR to be required – see Allison, 1999: 63), independent variables which are too highly correlated lead to incorrect conclusions about their effects on the dependent variable. The implication is that when we add independent variables, we should add those which are not likely to be highly correlated with each other, rather than those which we know will overlap significantly.

The conceptual framework for the multiple independent variable–one dependent variable type of study was shown in Chapter 1.

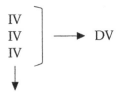

Examples can be found in almost any field of inquiry and some from different fields are shown in Box 7.1.

As pointed out in Chapter 6, we use multiple linear regression analysis to investigate the joint relationships involved here. We are interested in two main statistics which come from the regression analysis. The squared multiple correlation coefficient, R^2, tells us how much of the variance in the dependent variable we can account for with a particular set of independent variables. The standardised regression weight (β) tells us how much change we would make in the dependent variable by changing a particular independent variable. Therefore the regression weights tell us how important each independent variable is to the dependent variable. Section 7.4 of this chapter describes the logic of multiple linear regression analysis.

This sort of thinking has great power and wide applicability. Indeed, one reason this type of research design is so useful is that it models the way we think about the world. Consider, for example, the concepts of causality and explanation. We constantly seek to explain by trying to find the causes of different phenomena – for example, resistance to change, depression, vitamin use or behaviour problems (from the examples in Box 7.1). As explained in *Introduction to Social Research* (Punch, 1998: 78–83), the empirical research version of this is to explain the variation in the phenomenon in question or, in technical terms, to account for the variance in the dependent variable. Thus the question 'What causes academic achievement?' (or resistance to change or depression, and so on) is rephrased into 'How can we account for the variance in academic

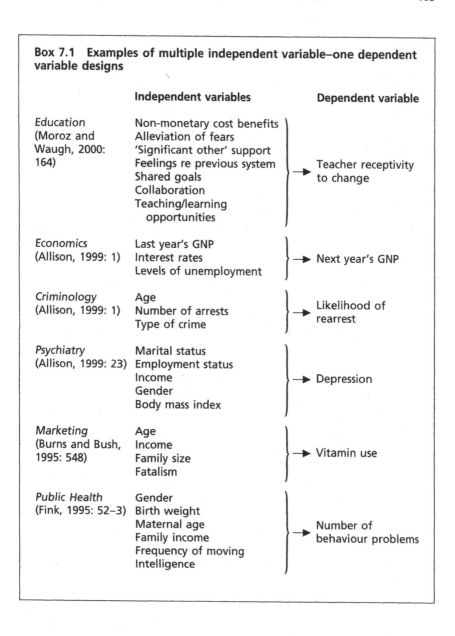

Box 7.1   Examples of multiple independent variable–one dependent variable designs

	Independent variables	Dependent variable
Education (Moroz and Waugh, 2000: 164)	Non-monetary cost benefits ⎱ Alleviation of fears ⎮ 'Significant other' support ⎮ Feelings re previous system ⎬ Shared goals ⎮ Collaboration ⎮ Teaching/learning ⎰ opportunities	→ Teacher receptivity to change
Economics (Allison, 1999: 1)	Last year's GNP ⎱ Interest rates ⎬ Levels of unemployment ⎰	→ Next year's GNP
Criminology (Allison, 1999: 1)	Age ⎱ Number of arrests ⎬ Type of crime ⎰	→ Likelihood of rearrest
Psychiatry (Allison, 1999: 23)	Marital status ⎱ Employment status ⎮ Income ⎬ Gender ⎮ Body mass index ⎰	→ Depression
Marketing (Burns and Bush, 1995: 548)	Age ⎱ Income ⎬ Family size ⎮ Fatalism ⎰	→ Vitamin use
Public Health (Fink, 1995: 52–3)	Gender ⎱ Birth weight ⎮ Maternal age ⎬ Family income ⎮ Frequency of moving ⎮ Intelligence ⎰	→ Number of behaviour problems

achievement?' (or resistance to change or depression, and so on). We then look for independent variables which can help account for that variance through their relationship with academic achievement. This is exactly the logic of the multiple independent variables–one dependent variable design. We account for variance in the dependent variable by knowing its relationship with different independent variables. The squared multiple correlation coefficient tells us how successful we are in accounting for variance in the dependent variable.

No doubt one reason we focus so much on the causes of things is to help us control and influence those things. If we know what causes failure (that is, poor academic achievement) in school or resistance to change or depression or the incidence and severity of cancer or obesity or road accidents, we can see where to direct our efforts in order to influence and change those things. The multiple-independent-variables–one-dependent-variable model gives us direct answers to this question of which independent variables are most important in affecting the dependent variable. The standardised regression weights tell us the importance of each independent variable.

This reasoning points to a general three-step research programme, using the multiple-independent-variables model of the quantitative survey.

- First, in a field of research, we select, as dependent variable for the research, something of great interest and importance, something we see as a problem and which we need to understand, and something we would then try to influence. In education, therefore, it is natural to select achievement as a dependent variable since it is both a key variable in education and typically the central mechanism education systems use for managing internal operations within the system, and external relationships with the occupational system. We want to understand it in order to improve it and perhaps also to reduce its variance. In other fields of social science, research concentrates similarly on accounting for the variance of major dependent variables.

- Secondly, we would select a set of independent variables which we expect to account for a substantial proportion of the dependent variable variance. In selecting these variables, we would be guided by the literature, previous research, experiential knowledge and theorising. We would also keep in mind the qualifications noted above regarding the relationship between the number of variables and sample size, and regarding multicollinearity among independent variables.

- Thirdly, using the methods described in this book for questionnaire development, sample selection and data collection, we measure the variables. After taking the analysis of the data through to the multiple regression stage, we would have the important statistics of R^2 and β.

We know, through R^2, what proportion of the variance in the dependent variable we can account for. This, in turn, tells us how far along we are in understanding the dependent variable. To repeat what was said in Chapter 6, an R^2 of 0.7 tells us we can account for some 70% of the variance in the dependent variable, and we are well on the way to understanding this particular dependent variable. If $R^2 = .10$, however, we know we have a long way to go in understanding this dependent variable. The squared multiple correlation coefficient, R^2, is like a sign-post or marker of our progress in understanding a particular dependent variable. It tells us whether we are zeroing in on the main factors which affect the variable or whether we need to change directions and look elsewhere, casting a wider net in our search for relevant independent variables.

Knowing the regression weights tells us where to concentrate our efforts in any attempt to change the dependent variable. Thus, if β for one independent variable is 0.45, we know that it is much more important than another variable whose β weight is, say, .05.[2]

I believe the importance of this three-part way of thinking in social science research should be stressed in our training of researchers. I believe also that it constitutes a neat package and a powerful and integrated research strategy, which is useful in a wide variety of situations. I think its logic is clear and can be easily understood: first we select dependent variables of importance; then we select independent variables likely to influence the dependent variable; then, using the quantitative survey methods described in this book, we measure these variables across a sample and use multiple regression analysis to investigate relationships. The R^2 tells us how close we are to a complete understanding of factors influencing the dependent variable. The βs tell us where to concentrate our efforts in order to bring about change in the dependent variable. We can use those results to guide subsequent research.

7.3   CONTROL VARIABLES

In introducing control variables, or covariates, we take a first step towards investigating, in detail, *how* the independent variables affect the dependent variable. The multiple independent variable model of section 7.2 tells us whether and to what extent different independent variables affect the dependent variable. It does not tell us how the independent variables affect the dependent variable. We can start on that by introducing control variables.

The second example of Chapter 6 used student alienation as a control variable. To control for a variable, as that term is used here, means to remove its effects. We often want to do this because we know that the independent variables are interrelated among each other, and therefore their effects on the dependent variable are somehow compounded. We want to know how a set of independent variables affects the dependent variable after controlling one or more other variables. This helps us to disentangle the effects of the independent variables on the dependent variable.

The general conceptual framework for that is

$$\text{IV} \longrightarrow \begin{bmatrix} \text{Control} \\ \text{variable} \end{bmatrix} \longrightarrow \text{DV}$$

Again, this clearly fits the quantitative survey strategy. The variables identified by the research questions and conceptual framework are measured across the sample, and then investigated for their relationship, in accordance with the research questions which follow from the conceptual framework.

It is worth stressing that all variables we want to use in a survey, including control variables, need to be measured. We cannot control a variable in the analysis of data without having measured it. I mention this because sometimes a researcher only realises the need to control for a variable during the data analysis stage. By that point, without measurements of the variable, it is too late – it cannot be done. This reinforces the desirability of careful planning before data collection.

Again, multiple linear regression analysis can be used as the data analysis technique for controlling variables. This time, as shown in Chapter 5, a simple sequence of two regression models or equations is involved. In the first, the control variable only is used to predict the dependent variable. In the second, the control variable is used together with the independent variables to predict the dependent variable. The difference between the two R^2s tells us the relationship between the independent and dependent variables after extracting (or controlling) the influence of the control variable.

This is analysis of covariance done by regression analysis. The control variable is the covariate. We covary out its influence on the dependent variable in order to see more clearly the role of the other independent variables – to see their effect on the dependent variable over and above the effects of the covariate.

As noted, introducing a control variable is a first step towards investigating how the independent variables affect the dependent variable. Further steps down that road take us towards path analysis, a technique for disentangling and quantifying networks of relationships among variables (see, for example, Blau and Duncan, 1967; Shipley, 2000).

7.4 MULTIPLE LINEAR REGRESSION ANALYSIS (MLR)

In *Introduction to Social Research* (Punch, 1998: 124–7), I stressed the value of multiple linear regression analysis (MLR) as a generalised design and data analysis strategy. Similarly, in this book (especially in Chapters 6 and 7), I have stressed MLR as a versatile and flexible technique for the analysis of quantitative survey data. In this section, I want to continue this emphasis and do three things:

- show the basic logic of the technique and the central ideas of regression and prediction;
- show how that basic logic translates into regression or prediction equations;
- show that both categorical and continuous variables can be dealt with in regression equations.

I want to keep this discussion on a logical level rather than go into technical details, including equations. The next book in this series will deal much more fully with the technical aspects of MLR.

1 Regression and prediction

A basic idea of regression analysis is that if two variables are related, we can use knowledge of one to predict the other. Conversely, if we can predict one variable from the other, the two variables are related. Thus 'relationships between variables' and 'prediction from one variable to another' are closely connected concepts. Throughout this book so far, I have written in terms of relationships between variables. But prediction is always implied by that expression. The prediction of a dependent variable from one or more independent variables is the central foundation of MLR. Regression analysis works on prediction.

Thus, when we ask if two variables are related, we are also asking, by implication, whether we can predict one from the other – more accurately, to what extent we can predict one from the other.[3] With measurements on the two variables for all members of the sample, we can set up a prediction equation to see how well we can predict one from the other. Then we work backwards from that result: if we can predict, the variables are related; if we cannot predict, the variables are not related.

2 Prediction equations

In line with this, MLR works basically by means of prediction equations. A regression equation is a prediction equation. In the most common case, we use the independent variables to predict the dependent variable.[4] This is why independent variables are sometimes called predictor variables and, when that terminology is used, the dependent variable is usually called the criterion variable. If we return to the simple example of Chapter 6, with two independent variables (MA, TT) and one dependent variable (achievement), the prediction equation here has MA and TT as predictor variables and achievement as criterion (or dependent) variable.

$$\begin{array}{cc}
\text{Independent} & \text{Dependent} \\
\text{(or predictor) variables} & \text{(or criterion) variable}
\end{array}$$

$$\begin{array}{ccc}
\text{Mental ability} \quad \text{Time on task} & \text{to predict} & \\
\text{MA} \quad + \quad \text{TT} & \Longrightarrow & \text{Achievement}
\end{array}$$

Since we have scores for all members of the sample on each of these three variables, we can use straightforward mathematics to solve the prediction equations and determine the weights for MA and TT, the independent variables.[5] Then we can assess how good the prediction is by calculating R^2. This tells us how much of the variance we can account for. In other words, it tells us how good our prediction is. The better the prediction, the more strongly the independent and dependent variables are related.

Furthermore, with R^2 as a measure of the predictive efficiency of a regression equation (telling us how well these independent variables predict this dependent variable – that is, how strongly these independent variables are related to this dependent variable), we can also compare the predictive efficiency of different regression equations. We can use this comparison to reach conclusions about whether adding independent variables increases to the predictability of the dependent variable.

3   Categorical and continuous variables

For many years in quantitative research, MLR was seen as applicable only to continuous variables. In the above example, MA and TT are continuous variables. In line with this, two main strands of statistical analysis techniques developed historically. With continuous variables there was the correlation-regression strand, including MLR. With categorical variables there was the analysis of variance (and covariance) strand. The latter was especially applicable to experimental design, where categorical variables are involved to show membership of the various experimental comparison groups.

Then came the realisation that both strands proceed from the same general linear model for statistical analysis. The strands are not really different, but rather different ways of interpreting and implementing that same general model. The application of this into research was first documented by Bottenber and Ward (1963), and has since been elaborated in several other books (for example, Kerlinger and Pedhazur, 1973; Allison, 1999; Kahane, 2001).

This means that we can include categorical variables in regression equations, and therefore we can use MLR to conduct analysis of variance and covariance. Therefore, I believe that MLR should be an important focus of statistical analysis training for quantitative survey research. An important bonus from this, in my experience, is that many students are more easily able to understand, appreciate and apply MLR, compared with understanding and applying traditional analysis of variance and covariance. A second bonus is that, once the basic logic and technical fundamentals are understood, researchers can build their own statistical models for the analysis of data, guided by the research questions and hypotheses of interest in their particular studies.

In other words, it is well worth learning MLR for its all-round value, especially for the type of quantitative-survey-relating-variables which has been the focus of this book. The fact that it can handle categorical and continuous variables – and thus we can use it to compare groups as well as to analyse relationships among continuous variables – adds to its versatility and applicability. Because of this, and because of its central role in studying relationships between variables (both categorical and continuous), it will be the focus of the next book in this series.

7.5 REVIEW CONCEPTS

multiple independent variables
accounting for variance
control variables
analysis of covariance
multiple linear regression
regression and prediction
prediction equations
squared multiple correlation coefficient, R^2
(standardised partial) regression weight, β

NOTES

1. In the limit, if we went all the way to the absurd situation where the number of variables in a study is equal to the sample size, R^2 would equal 1.0, by definition. The result would be meaningless – it

certainly does not mean that we can explain 100% of the variance in the dependent variable. The closer we get to this limiting situation, the more our result becomes meaningless.

2. We can test the statistical significance of regression weights – that is, whether they are significantly different from zero (Allison, 1999).

3. We are really asking whether we can predict better than chance. Statistical significance testing helps us answer that question.

4. In the analysis of covariance case above, we also use the control variable as a predictor.

5. The solution is found by choosing the weights according to the restriction that the correlation between predicted and actual scores on the criterion variable is maximised. This restriction enables solutions to the equations.

Appendix 1

Further Reading on Technical Topics

The literature on quantitative research methodology is extensive. Much of it is written within particular social science areas, but some is more generic across social science. The literature ranges from moderately technical to extremely technical. This can be a problem in quantitative research training, since mathematics lies underneath these technical topics and provides the theoretical foundations for them. As a result, some of the extremely technical literature requires high levels of mathematical knowledge. For that reason, I have concentrated in the readings selected here on moderately technical literature. Some mathematics is inevitably involved in the six topics listed below, but the central ideas in each case can also be understood aside from the mathematics.

1. SAMPLING AND SAMPLE SIZE

Black, Thomas R. (1999) *Doing Quantitative Research in the Social Sciences: An Integrated Approach to Research Design, Measurement and Statistics*. London: Sage, pp. 110–39.

Burns, Robert B. (1994) *Introduction to Research Methods*. Melbourne: Longman, pp. 61–82.

Crowl, T.K. (1993) *Fundamentals of Educational Research*. Dubuque, IA: Wm C. Brown, pp. 280–9.

de Vaus, D.A. (1991) *Surveys in Social Research*, 3rd edn. St Leonards, NSW: Allen & Unwin, pp. 60–79.

Dooley, D. (1984) *Social Research Methods*. Englewood Cliffs, NJ: Prentice-Hall, pp. 245–51.

Edwards, Jack E., Thomas, Marie D., Rosenfeld, Paul and Booth-Kewley, Stephanie (1997) *How to Conduct Organizational Surveys: A Step-by-Step Guide*. Thousand Oaks, CA: Sage, pp. 5–65.

Fraenkel, J.R. and Wallen, N.E. (1990) *How to Design and Evaluate Research in Education*. New York: McGraw-Hill, pp. 66–87.

Gay, L.R. (1992) *Educational Research: Competencies for Analysis and Application*, 4th edn. New York: Macmillan, pp. 123–45.

Kidder, L.H. and Judd, C.M. with Smith, E.R. (1986) *Research Methods in Social Relations*, 5th edn. New York: Holt, Rinehart & Winston, pp. 143–67.

Moser, C.A. and Kalton, G. (1979) *Survey Methods in Social Investigation*, 2nd edn. Aldershot: Gower, pp. 61–210.

Tuckman, B.W. (1999) *Conducting Educational Research*, 5th edn. Fort Worth, TX: Harcourt Brace, pp. 258–62.

Wallen, N.E. and Fraenkel, J.R. (1991) *Educational Research: A Guide to the Process.* New York: McGraw-Hill, pp. 126–57.

2. MULTIPLE-ITEM SCALES

Black, Thomas R. (1999) *Doing Quantitative Research in the Social Sciences: An Integrated Approach to Research Design, Measurement and Statistics.* London: Sage, pp. 227–33.

Burns, Robert B. (1994) *Introduction to Research Methods.* Melbourne: Longman, pp. 332–43.

Crowl, T.K. (1993) *Fundamentals of Educational Research.* Dubuque, IA: Wm C. Brown, pp. 309–16.

de Vaus, D.A. (1991) *Surveys in Social Research*, 3rd edn. St Leonards, NSW: Allen & Unwin, pp. 249–75.

Edwards, Jack E., Thomas, Marie D., Rosenfeld, Paul and Booth-Kewley, Stephanie (1997) *How to Conduct Organizational Surveys: A Step-by-Step Guide.* Thousand Oaks, CA: Sage, pp. 43–6.

Kidder, L.H. and Judd, C.M. with Smith, E.R. (1986) *Research Methods in Social Relations*, 5th edn. New York: Holt, Rinehart & Winston, pp. 191–218.

Oppenheim, A.N. (1992) *Questionnaire Design, Interviewing and Attitude Measurement*, new edition. London: Pinter, pp. 195–200.

Spector, Paul E. (1992) *Summated Rating Scale Construction: An Introduction.* Newbury Park, CA: Sage.

Tuckman, B.W. (1999) *Conducting Educational Research*, 5th edn. Fort Worth, TX: Harcourt Brace, pp. 216–20.

Wallen, N.E. and Fraenkel, J.R. (1991) *Educational Research: A Guide to the Process.* New York: McGraw-Hill, pp. 79–85.

3. RELIABILITY (INCLUDING COEFFICIENT ALPHA)

Black, Thomas R. (1999) *Doing Quantitative Research in the Social Sciences: An Integrated Approach to Research Design, Measurement and Statistics.* London: Sage, pp. 195–9, 273–98.

Burns, Robert B. (1994) *Introduction to Research Methods.* Melbourne: Longman, pp. 203–17.

Crowl, T.K. (1993) *Fundamentals of Educational Research.* Dubuque, IA: Wm C. Brown, pp. 290–9.

Dooley, D. (1984) *Social Research Methods.* Englewood Cliffs, NJ: Prentice-Hall, pp. 59–66.

Fraenkel, J.R. and Wallen, N.E. (1990) *How to Design and Evaluate Research in Education.* New York: McGraw-Hill, pp. 133–41.

Gay, L.R. (1992) *Educational Research: Competencies for Analysis and Application*, 4th edn. New York: Macmillan, pp. 161–70.

Mehrens, W.A. and Lehmann, I.J. (1984) *Measurement and Evaluation in Education and Psychology*, 3rd edn. New York: Holt, Rinehart & Winston, p. 277.

Oppenheim, A.N. (1992) *Questionnaire Design, Interviewing and Attitude Measurement*, new edition. London: Pinter, pp. 159–66.

Sax, G. (1989) *Principles of Educational and Psychological Measurement and Evaluation*, 3rd edn. Belmont, CA: Wadsworth, pp. 265–9, 614–15.

Tuckman, B.W. (1999) *Conducting Educational Research*, 5th edn. Fort Worth, TX: Harcourt Brace, pp. 198–200.

Wallen, N.E. and Fraenkel, J.R. (1991) *Educational Research: A Guide to the Process*. New York: McGraw-Hill, pp. 87–95.

4. VALIDITY

Black, Thomas R. (1999) *Doing Quantitative Research in the Social Sciences: An Integrated Approach to Research Design, Measurement and Statistics*. London: Sage, pp. 191–5, 219–24, 298–302.

Burns, Robert B. (1994) *Introduction to Research Methods*. Melbourne: Longman, pp. 217–28.

Crowl, T.K. (1993) *Fundamentals of Educational Research*. Dubuque, IA: Wm C. Brown, pp. 299–304.

Dooley, D. (1984) *Social Research Methods*. Englewood Cliffs, NJ: Prentice-Hall, pp. 66–74.

Fraenkel, J.R. and Wallen, N.E. (1990) *How to Design and Evaluate Research in Education*. New York: McGraw Hill, pp. 126–33.

Gay, L.R. (1992) *Educational Research: Competencies for Analysis and Application*, 4th edn. New York: Macmillan, pp. 155–61.

Oppenheim, A.N. (1992) *Questionnaire Design, Interviewing and Attitude Measurement*, new edition. London: Pinter, pp. 160–6.

Tuckman, B.W. (1999) *Conducting Educational Research*, 5th edn. Fort Worth, TX: Harcourt Brace, pp. 200–2.

Wallen, N.E. and Fraenkel, J.R. (1991) *Educational Research: A Guide to the Process*. New York: McGraw-Hill, pp. 95–104.

5. ANALYSIS OF DATA

(a) t test

Black, Thomas R. (1999) *Doing Quantitative Research in the Social Sciences: An Integrated Approach to Research Design, Measurement and Statistics*. London: Sage, pp. 406–40.

Burns, Robert B. (1994) *Introduction to Research Methods*. Melbourne: Longman, pp. 139–48.

Crowl, T.K. (1993) *Fundamentals of Educational Research*. Dubuque, IA: Wm C. Brown, pp. 359–61.

Fraenkel, J.R. and Wallen, N.E. (1990) *How to Design and Evaluate Research in Education*. New York: McGraw-Hill, pp. 185–6.

Gay, L.R. (1992) *Educational Research: Competencies for Analysis and Application*, 4th edn. New York: Macmillan, pp. 445–52.

Rosenberg, K.M. (1990) *Statistics for the Behavioural Sciences*. Dubuque, IA: Wm C. Brown, pp. 220–41.

(b)   Analysis of Variance (Anova)

Black, Thomas R. (1999) *Doing Quantitative Research in the Social Sciences: An Integrated Approach to Research Design, Measurement and Statistics*. London: Sage, pp. 441–83.

Fraenkel, J.R. and Wallen, N.E. (1990) *How to Design and Evaluate Research in Education*. New York: McGraw-Hill, p. 186.

Gay, L.R. (1992) *Educational Research: Competencies for Analysis and Application*, 4th edn. New York: Macmillan, pp. 452–8.

Rosenberg, K.M. (1990) *Statistics for the Behavioural Sciences*. Dubuque, IA: Wm C. Brown, pp. 308–46.

Tuckman, B.W. (1999) *Conducting Educational Research*, 5th edn. Fort Worth, TX: Harcourt Brace, pp. 306–12.

6.   STATISTICAL SIGNIFICANCE

Black, Thomas R. (1999) *Doing Quantitative Research in the Social Sciences: An Integrated Approach to Research Design, Measurement and Statistics*. London: Sage, pp. 337–400.

Burns, Robert B. (1994) *Introduction to Research Methods*. Melbourne: Longman, pp. 46–60.

Crowl, T.K. (1993) *Fundamentals of Educational Research*. Dubuque, IA: Wm C. Brown, pp. 253–68.

Dooley, D. (1984) *Social Research Methods*. Englewood Cliffs, NJ: Prentice-Hall, pp. 102–18.

Fraenkel, J.R. and Wallen, N.E. (1990) *How to Design and Evaluate Research in Education*. New York: McGraw-Hill, pp. 186, 172–93.

Gay, L.R. (1992) *Educational Research: Competencies for Analysis and Application*, 4th edn. New York: Macmillan, pp. 423–45.

Tuckman, B.W. (1999) *Conducting Educational Research*, 5th edn. Fort Worth, TX: Harcourt Brace, pp. 282–6.

A Two-Variable Quantitative Survey: Socio-Economic Status (SES) and Alienation from School

As a separate project, this two-variable quantitative survey can be set up using the headings described earlier. Thus:

Area

Students' reactions to school.

Topic

SES and alienation from school.

General research question

What is the relationship between SES and student alienation from school?

Specific research questions

1 What is the distribution of SES across this sample?
2 What is the distribution of alienation across this sample?
3 What is the relationship between SES and alienation?

Conceptual framework

Independent variable   Dependent variable
SES $\longrightarrow$ Alienation

Measuring the variables

As before, the variables SES and alienation need to be measured, and the earlier comments and instruments (Chapter 6) for both variables apply here.

Sample

It is important to ensure variability in the independent variable SES and also to take into account the variables gender and age in the sample plan. They can either be controlled in the sample (for example, by selecting only either boys or girls, or by selecting say, only, 15 year olds) or allowed to vary in the sample and taken into account in the analysis. The latter strategy increases the number of variables and therefore the desired sample size.

Data collection and analysis

These would proceed as before, and the data for specific research questions (1) and (2) would be presented in distribution tables, showing the mean, standard deviation and score range for each variable (see Chapter 6, pp. 88, 95).

Specific research question (3) concerns the SES–alienation relationship. If we categorise SES into three levels, a table can summarise the data, of this form:

SES category	Alienation level (mean of each group)
High	
Medium	
Low	

Additionally, with SES and alienation scored as continuous variables, we can plot the variables against each other as a scatter diagram (Punch, 1998: 132) to see their relationship more clearly than the above table shows. That would give rise to the four general possibilities shown below.

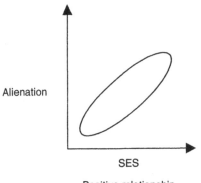

This scatter diagram shows a positive relationship – higher levels of SES are associated with higher levels of alienation, and lower levels of SES are associated with lower levels of alienation.

Positive relationship

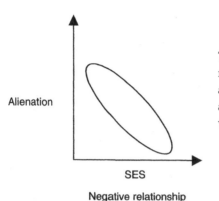

This scatter diagram shows a negative relationship – higher levels of SES are associated with lower levels of alienation, and lower levels of SES with higher levels of alienation.

Negative relationship

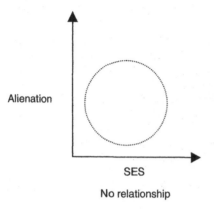

This scatter diagram shows no relationship – any particular level of SES may be associated with both higher and lower levels of alienation.

No relationship

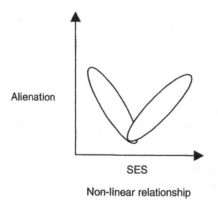

This scatter diagram shows a curvilinear relationship – lower levels of SES are associated with higher levels of alienation, medium levels of SES are associated with lower levels of alienation, and higher levels of SES are again associated with higher levels of alienation.

Non-linear relationship

The last possibility is often seen in research data on this topic and is used to support the theory that, since schools are typically middle-class institutions, the compatibility between school and home environments is greater for students from middle-class homes, resulting in lower levels of alienation.

References

Allison, Paul D. (1999) *Multiple Regression: A Primer*. Thousand Oaks, CA: Pine Forge.

Alreck, Pamela L. and Settle, Robert B. (1995) *The Survey Research Handbook*. Chicago: Irwin.

Babbie, Earl (1990) *Survey Research Methods*, 2nd edn. Belmont, CA: Wadsworth.

Bardsley, W.N. (1976) *Student Alienation and Commitment to School: A Multi-Variate Analysis of the Effects of Home and School Environments*. Unpublished PhD thesis, Australian National University.

Bearden, W.O. and Netemeyer, R.G. (1999) *Handbook of Marketing Scales: Multi-Item Measures for Marketing and Consumer Behaviour Research*, 2nd edn. Thousand Oaks, CA: Sage.

Black, Thomas R. (1999) *Doing Quantitative Research in the Social Sciences: An Integrated Approach to Research Design, Measurement and Statistics*. London: Sage.

Blau, P.M. and Duncan, O.D. (1967) *The American Occupational Structure*. New York: Wiley.

Bottenber, R.A. and Ward, J.H. (1963) *Applied Multiple Linear Regression*. Texas: Airforce Systems Command.

Braverman, Marc T. and Slater, Jana Kay (1996) *Advances in Survey Research*. San Francisco: Jossey-Bass.

Burns, Alvin C. and Bush, Ronald F. (1995) *Marketing Research*. Englewood Cliffs, NJ: Prentice-Hall.

Burns, Robert B. (1994) *Introduction to Research Methods*. Melbourne: Longman.

Converse, J.M. and Presser, S. (1986) *Survey Questions: Handcrafting the Standardised Questionnaire*. Beverly Hills, CA: Sage.

Crowl, T.K. (1993) *Fundamentals of Educational Research*. Dubuque, IA: Wm C. Brown.

Czaja, Ronald and Blair, Johnny (1996) *Designing Surveys: A Guide to Decisions and Procedures*. Thousand Oaks, CA: Pine Forge.

de Vaus, D.A. (1991) *Surveys in Social Research*, 3rd edn. St Leonards, NSW: Allen & Unwin.

Dillman, Don A. (1999) *Mail and Internet Surveys: The Tailored Design Method*, 3rd edn. New York: John Wiley & Sons.

Dooley, D. (1984) *Social Research Methods*. Englewood Cliffs, NJ: Prentice-Hall.

Edwards, Jack E., Thomas, Marie D., Rosenfeld, Paul and Booth-Kewley, Stephanie (1997) *How to Conduct Organizational Surveys: A Step-by-Step Guide*. Thousand Oaks, CA: Sage.

Fink, Arlene (1995) *How to Ask Survey Questions.* Thousand Oaks, CA: Sage.

Fink, Arlene and Kosecoff, Jacqueline (1998) *How to Conduct Surveys: A Step-by-Step Guide.* Thousand Oaks, CA: Sage.

Fraenkel, J.R. and Wallen, N.E. (1990) *How to Design and Evaluate Research in Education.* New York: McGraw-Hill.

Gay, L.R. (1992) *Educational Research: Competencies for Analysis and Application,* 4th edn. New York: Macmillan.

Hart, C. (1998) *Doing a Literature Review: Releasing the Social Science Research Imagination.* London: Sage.

Hart, C. (2001) *Doing a Literature Search: A Comprehensive Guide for the Social Sciences.* London: Sage.

Kahane, L.H. (2001) *Regression Basics.* Thousand Oaks, CA: Sage.

Kendall, Patricia and Lazarsfeld, Paul F. (1950) 'Problems of survey analysis', in Robert Merton and Paul Lazarsfeld (eds), *Continuities in Social Research: Studies in the Scope and Method of the American Soldier.* New York: The Free Press.

Kerlinger, F.N. and Pedhazur, E.J. (1973) *Multiple Regression in Behavioural Research.* New York: Holt, Rinehart & Winston.

Kidder, L.H. and Judd, C.M. with Smith, E.R. (1986) *Research Methods in Social Relations,* 5th edn. New York: Holt, Rinehart & Winston.

Krueger, R.A. (1994) *Focus Groups: A Practical Guide for Applied Research.* Thousand Oaks, CA: Sage.

Lewins, F. (1992) *Social Science Methodology.* Melbourne: Macmillan.

Mehrens, W.A. and Lehmann, I.J. (1984) *Measurement and Evaluation in Education and Psychology,* 3rd edn. New York: Holt, Rinehart & Winston.

Merton, Robert and Lazarsfeld, Paul (eds) (1950) *Continuities in Social Research: Studies in the Scope and Method of the American Soldier.* New York: The Free Press.

Miller, Delbert D. (1991) *Handbook of Research Design and Social Measurement,* 5th edn. Newbury Park, CA: Sage.

Morgan, D.L. (1988) *Focus Groups as Qualitative Research.* Newbury Park, CA: Sage.

Moroz, R. and Waugh, R.F. (2000) 'Teacher receptivity to system-wide educational Change', *Journal of Educational Administration,* 38 (2): 159–78.

Moser, C.A. and Kalton, G. (1979) *Survey Methods in Social Investigation,* 2nd edn. Aldershot: Gower.

Oppenheim, A.N. (1992) *Questionnaire Design, Interviewing and Attitude Measurement,* new edition. London: Pinter.

Punch, Keith F. (1998) *Introduction to Social Research: Quantitative and Qualitative Approaches.* London: Sage.

Punch, Keith F. (2000) *Developing Effective Research Proposals.* London: Sage.

Rosenberg, K.M. (1990) *Statistics for the Behavioural Sciences.* Dubuque, IA: Wm C. Brown.

Rosenberg, Morris (1968) *The Logic of Survey Analysis.* New York: Basic Books.

Sapsford, Roger (1999) *Survey Research.* London: Sage.

Sax, G. (1989) *Principles of Educational and Psychological Measurement and Evaluation,* 3rd edn. Belmont, CA: Wadsworth.

Schofield, William (1996) 'Survey sampling', in Roger Sapsford and Victor Jupp (eds), *Data Collection and Analysis.* London: Sage, pp. 25–6.

Sheridan, B.E. (1976) *Reference Group Influences on the Aspirations of Adolescents.* Unpublished MEd thesis, The University of Western Australia.

Shipley, B. (2000) *Cause and Correlation in Biology: A User's Guide to Path Analysis, Structural Equations and Causal Inference.* Cambridge: Cambridge University Press.

Siegel, Sidney (1956) *Nonparametric Statistics for the Behavioural Sciences.* New York: McGraw-Hill.

Spector, Paul E. (1992) *Summated Rating Scale Construction: An Introduction.* Newbury Park, CA: Sage.

Stewart, D. and Shamdasani, P. (1990) *Focus Groups: Theory and Practice.* Newbury Park, CA: Sage.

Stouffer, Samuel A. et al. (1949) *The American Soldier.* Princeton, NJ: Princeton University Press.

Sudman, S. and Bradburn, N.M. (1982) *Asking Questions: A Practical Guide to Questionnaire Design.* San Francisco: Jossey-Bass.

Suskie, L. (1996) *Questionnaire Survey Research: What Works.* Tallahasse, FL: Association for Institutional Research.

Tuckman, B.W. (1999) *Conducting Educational Research*, 5th edn. Fort Worth, TX: Harcourt Brace.

Wallen, N.E. and Fraenkel, J.R. (1991) *Educational Research: A Guide to the Process.* New York: McGraw-Hill.

Index

Lightning Source UK Ltd.
Milton Keynes UK
UKOW06f1719100516

273980UK00002B/169/P